THEATRE'S STRANGEST ACTS

Other titles in this series:

THEATRE'S STRANGEST ACTS

EXTRAORDINARY BUT TRUE TALES FROM THE HISTORY OF THEATRE

Sheridan Morley

ROBSON

First published in the United Kingdom in 2005 by
Robson Books
151 Freston Road
London
W10 6TH

An imprint of Anova Books Company Ltd

ISBN 1 86105 674 5

A CIP catalogue record for this book is available from the British Library

10 9 8 7 6 5 4 3 2 1

Typeset by SX Composing DTP, Rayleigh, Essex
Printed and bound by MPG Books Ltd, Bodmin, Cornwall

This book can be ordered direct from the publisher
Contact the marketing department, but try your bookshop first

www.anovabooks.com

Contents

THE GREEKS

ATHENS, 534 BC

Nothing changes. In the highly competitive world of West End and Broadway theatre, amid the arguments about funding and casting, and the audience complaints that the plays are too long, too short, too serious, not serious enough, too political, too musical, too difficult or too idiotic, spare a thought for the Greeks. Theatre as we know it, with actors, scripts, and the rest, started as a competition, the Great Dionysia. Every year in Athens, at a specially built auditorium near the Temple of Dionysis, three playwrights (the Greek word originally meant 'teacher') were pitched against one another. Each had to write, produce and perform not one but four plays, three tragedies (the word 'tragedy' meant 'goat-song' but nobody knows why) and a satyr play, known collectively as a tetralogy.

Up to 20,000 people (all men) crammed into the auditorium (supposed to seat only 14,000) each spring for the biggest annual gathering in the Greek world: the entire male population would turn up to see the plays as well as to receive honours and celebrate their good fortune. Greek architects perfected a method of design that allowed a word to be spoken on the stage and heard at the back of the enormous auditorium, a trick that has never been replicated in our own time.

Drama means a 'doing', or an 'enactment', so the actors couldn't just speak to the audience as in a poetry reading, but also had to move, sing, dance and interact with each other. Greek drama used ancient myths and stories, all with female characters, although, of course, there were no female actors.

1

The actors played Gods and kings, with a traditional background of a chorus, who were the narrators, storytellers representing the common people.

Drama flourished in the fifth century BC and many playwrights competed for the honour of the first prize. But there were three who competed against one another in the Great Dionysia whose work we still see performed in our own theatres – and all three died in a strange manner. They lived in an Athens devoted to the competition of the plays and the individuality of expression.

Aeschylus (c. 525–456 BC) was the first. He began competing in 499 BC and won his first victory in 484 BC, eventually winning a total of thirteen competitions with thirteen tetralogies. He may have written as many as ninety plays; the titles of 83 have come down to us, with seven plays and many fragments surviving. The *Oresteia* is the only surviving trilogy of Greek tragedies that we know were produced together.

Sophocles (496–406 BC) was the golden boy of Greek theatre. Charming and handsome, a prodigious lover of men and women, a politician, soldier and ambassador, as well as a great personal friend of the ruler, Pericles, he boasted a popularity such that, in the weeks prior to his first playwriting competition, excitement in Athens reached fever pitch. To prevent a riot, the panel of judges had to be replaced by a council of generals. Sophocles was awarded first prize at the competition, even defeating Aeschylus.

His success as a playwright was not, however, matched by his skills as an actor: while most dramatists took part in their own productions, Sophocles was forced to abandon the stage when audiences complained that his voice was thin and reedy. Although he completed more than 120 tragedies, only seven survive, of which *Antigone* is the earliest.

Euripides (480–406 BC) was a different kettle of fish altogether. He wrote about real people and their problems, even though his stories, like those of his compatriots, were of heroes and victories. In his own lifetime, he was the least successful of the three men, winning first prize at the Dionysia only four times. Yet more of his plays have survived than those written by Aeschylus and Sophocles combined.

He was undoubtedly the bad boy of Greek tragedy, and his plays are modern in a way that those of Aeschylus and Sophocles are not – he was an acute observer of human nature, and the father of the psychological drama. Sophocles said that, while he himself depicted men as they ought to be, Euripides depicted them as they really are. Euripides is arguably the darkest and most disturbing of the Greek playwrights. He questions authority and is fascinated by the oppressed: women, barbarians and slaves are more than just background on the Euripidean stage. His was the unwanted voice of conscience in his age – a man unafraid to point out the lies with which a civilisation comforts itself. He was not, of course, very popular with his fellow Athenians. In the end, the frenzied descent into chaos he so often imagined was truest to Athens's fate. Infighting and dirty politics compromised the city's good name, and Athens fell to her hated enemy, Sparta, just a few years after Euripides's death.

All three playwrights met improbable fates, Aeschylus's being the most bizarre. He died aged 68 in Gela, Sicily, where he spent time at the request of a friendly tyrant, Hieron. It was said that an eagle grasping a tortoise flew high into the air and, mistaking Aeschylus's bald head for a rock, accidentally dropped the tortoise on his head, killing him.

Sophocles lived to a great old age, ninety, which was almost unheard of in the fifth century BC. Shortly before his death, his son, Iophon, took him to court, claiming that his father was too mentally infirm to manage his own affairs. Sophocles decided to prove his sanity by reciting a portion of *Oedipus at Colonus*, which he was composing at the time. 'If I am Sophocles,' he said, 'I am not senile, and if I am senile, I am not Sophocles.' The court was so moved by his recitation that the case was immediately dismissed but soon after, flushed with his success in court, and giving an ill-advised public reading of *Antigone*, he tried and failed to recite a fatally long sentence in a single breath. Rather than take a breath in the middle of a sentence, he expired on the spot. Not a bad way for a poet to go.

And poor old Euripides? He, as usual, got the worst of it. In 408 BC, feeling unloved and unwanted by his fellow Athenians, and having lost the Dionysia yet again, he left Athens for the court of King Archelaus of Macedon and there wrote his masterpiece, *The Bacchae*. The story of his death in 406 BC, the same year as that of Sophocles, is probably a myth but a compelling one, as it gained currency among the Athenians and gives an insight into what they thought of him. A vengeful woman, whether a mistress or a wife is unknown, is said to have set a pack of wild dogs on him and they tore him to shreds.

As a postscript, after his death his son brought Euripides's last three plays, including *The Bacchae*, back to Athens for production. There, at the Great Dionysia, the same festival where Euripides had lost to now-forgotten playwrights so many times, *The Bacchae* and its companion pieces won first prize.

THE MYSTERIOUS DEATH AND AFTERLIFE OF CHRISTOPHER MARLOWE

ELEANOR BULL'S ROOMING HOUSE, 1593

Of all the pretenders to the throne of Shakespeare, by far the most exciting is Christopher Marlowe. As a playwright, Kit Marlowe was the first to use English blank verse, later taken up by Shakespeare, and both playwrights were writing for the same company of actors, the Strange company, at the same time. They were friends, colleagues, and, as was the custom of the time, they stole from anywhere they could whenever they could get away with it. The influence of one upon the other is obvious in the writings of them both. But is there a stranger story to explain that?

Born on 6 February 1564, the eldest son of a Canterbury shoemaker, Marlowe was from all accounts a brilliant scholar. The Archbishop of Canterbury himself picked him out as a deserving boy and provided a scholarship to Cambridge University, clearly intending to groom him for a high-flying career in the church. But Kit had other ideas.

As soon as he completed his education in 1587, he moved to London to be the dramatist for an acting company of the Lords Strange and Admiral – the Admiral's Men. Marlowe's most significant plays – *The Jew of Malta*, *Tamburlaine the Great*, *Edward the Second* and *The Tragical History of Doctor Faustus* – were all written between 1587 and 1593, along with a number of poems, dramatic odes, political reports, translations from

Latin and what we might today call journalism. His most ambitious work was the heroic epic *Tamburlaine the Great*, a play in two parts, of five acts each. This was composed in poetic form, which was not unusual, but it had the distinction of being the first play written in English blank verse. Where Marlowe led, Shakespeare followed.

But Kit was more, much more, than just a writer. He was one of the brightest lights of his generation, although Shakespeare's literary prestige eclipsed his during their lifetimes and has far outstripped him since their deaths. Much of what we know about him is, at least, highly coloured and often unreliable, but then he was one of the most colourful characters of his age, with a finger in many pies.

He was certainly both a spy and a common criminal. He was, for example, expelled from Holland for counterfeiting gold coins. As early as 1580, when Kit was only sixteen, he took leave from his studies in Cambridge to take on a secret mission for the Queen and, for the rest of his life, whenever he got into hot water, he would be mysteriously released by intercession from 'on high'. In 1589 he was charged with the murder of William Bradley and sent to Newgate Prison, but was acquitted after two weeks. It was not the last time the quick-tempered author was arrested and jailed, however: in 1592 an injunction was brought against him because of a street fight in which a man was killed. He got off that one, too.

Marlowe dabbled in alchemy, reportedly converted to Catholicism, was openly homosexual, even writing a same-sex affair into his *Edward II* at a time when suggesting a monarch was or could be guilty of what was seen as deviant sexual activity – and, remember, the monarch at the time was the Virgin Queen herself, Elizabeth I, whose affairs were many and notorious – was treason. He had powerful enemies but, for most of his life, even more powerful friends, such as Sir Walter Raleigh and Sir Francis Walsingham, head of the secret service, whose brother was probably one of Marlowe's lovers.

He was accused of atheism, blasphemy, subversion and black magic, and, finally, it was the charge of atheism that might have done for him if the authorities had been able to find him. The rumours had become too insistent to be ignored. The agents of the Queen's Privy Council went to his lodgings to arrest him yet again. He was out, so they took his friend and roommate, Thomas Kyd, and tried to get him to incriminate Marlowe. Under torture, Kyd declared that a document in their apartments denying the divinity of Christ belonged to Marlowe (see also 'Thomas Kyd and the Bridewell').

Two notorious sayings, either of which would have been grounds for arrest, and famously attributed to Marlowe by a contemporary, were, 'St John the Evangelist was bedfellow to Christ and leaned always in his bosom, that he used him as the sinners of Sodoma' – in other words, that Christ himself was a homosexual – and 'they that love not Tobacco & Boies [boys] are fooles'. Even then, none of this got to the Teflon Marlowe.

Many have complained that Kit never left an authentic autograph, nor a folio so that his work could be authenticated, and never had his work published. Many of his existing works are in fragments, and proving he wrote them is difficult if not impossible.

But why should he have done so? He was only 29 years old on 30 May 1593, and had every reason to believe he would live long enough to write much more. He was in considerable trouble, certainly, but his friends and his quick wits had always saved him before, and surely would again. Yes, he was ducking the Privy Council, but a man needed to eat, and he had a meeting with three of his friends, all dodgy, and all connected, as he was, to the secret service.

They met at a lodging house above a tavern in Deptford, owned by Eleanor Bull. In addition to Kit, there were Ingram Frizer, a known con artist and moneylender, Nicholas Skeres, a fence and Frizer's frequent accomplice, and Robert Poley, an occasional courier/spy for Her Majesty's secret service, who had boasted of his ability to lie convincingly under any circumstances.

Exactly what happened that night is still unclear, despite hundreds of scholarly papers and forensic investigations, but sometime after the four friends and co-conspirators had consumed a good deal of food and drink, a brawl broke out between them and, by the end of it, Marlowe was dead, stabbed through the eye. His killer, Frizer, was quickly pardoned by the Queen on grounds of self-defence, and his employers did not fire or take any other action against him.

According to the records of the coroner's inquest, Marlowe and his friend Ingram Frizer had begun to wrangle over payment of the bill. Marlowe wrenched Frizer's dagger from its sheath, and struck him twice about the head with it. In the struggle Frizer got the dagger. 'And so it befell, in that affray,' the official record tells us, 'that the said Ingram, in the defence of his life, with the dagger aforesaid of the value of twelve pence, gave the said Christopher a mortal wound above his right eye.'

But what really happened? Was he murdered on the orders of the Earl of Essex, the Queen's current lover? Or was his death ordered by foreign powers who thought he knew too much? Or was the deed commissioned by a gay nobleman fearful that Marlowe's recklessness would result in the unmasking of his sexuality? Then again, could this have been political murder organised by Sir Francis Walsingham, whose man Frizer was following an adventure that had gone wrong.

Most intriguingly, was Kit really dead? Because of the timing of his death and the lack of retribution against the killer, some scholars believe that the playwright's demise was faked and that he took up a new identity. But why? There are several possibilities, including a desire to escape the Privy Council and a wish to engage in further spying activities for Walsingham.

But could this new identity be that of William Shakespeare? It is certainly true that Shakespeare's greatest works were created after the 'death' of Christopher Marlowe. Kit had the education that Shakespeare did not and had travelled widely all over Europe on spy business and was therefore familiar with settings for the plays, settings such as Venice and Verona, where Shakespeare never went. He was himself a brilliant playwright and would have known the Elizabethan theatrical territory through which Shakespeare had to navigate. Suppose, just suppose, that Shakespeare was, after all, just a middle-class grammar school boy from Stratford-on-Avon who became an actor and then a figurehead for the political ne'er-do-well, Christopher Marlowe.

The records show that Christopher Marlowe was buried in the churchyard at St Nicholas's, Deptford, three days after the brawl that killed him.

Maybe . . .

THOMAS KYD AND THE BRIDEWELL

CITY OF LONDON, 1594

The theatre has its share of happy breaks and dazzling careers but it also has plenty of incidences of bad luck, of talent unfulfilled, of wrong turnings . . . One such, which came to a brief and bloody end, was that of the playwright Thomas Kyd, who was born in London in 1558, but died broken and destitute at the age of 36 (which was young, even by Elizabethan standards) in December 1594. The man laid to rest in a poor man's grave should have been wealthy, successful and alive. What went wrong?

Hardly remembered today outside academic circles, in his time Kyd was at least as important a writer as his friends, Marlowe and Shakespeare, and he should have lived to leave a similar legacy.

Kyd was the author of several influential plays, including the enormously popular *Spanish Tragedy* (1589), with its gallons of onstage blood, and *Hamlet* (c. 1587), not to be confused with Shakespeare's famous play of 1603. However, when Shakespeare wrote his version of the story of the Danish prince, *his* play drew heavily (not least in its title and central character) on the Thomas Kyd play, which is referred to today by scholars as the '*Ur Hamlet*'.

Kyd's *Hamlet* and Shakespeare's have some obvious similarities: the plot involves death and double-dealings at a foreign court; it has a central figure (a murder victim) called Horatio, and a character who, like Hamlet, seeks revenge for his relative's death and does so while pretending to be mad.

10

There's also a play within a play, during which in Kyd's case the villains are murdered, whereas in Shakespeare's version Hamlet's guilty stepfather, Claudius, merely watches a play that mirrors his own crime. Both plays were based on, and inspired by, Seneca's Roman tragedies.

Moving as of right among the theatrical elite, Kyd shared rooms with his friend, the playwright Christopher Marlowe (the writer of such classic plays as *Tamburlaine, Edward II, Doctor Faustus* and *The Jew of Malta*), who also met an early death. Indeed, the two deaths were probably (though unprovably) related. And that, as it turned out, was probably Kyd's problem. In his association with Christopher Marlowe he flew too near the sun like the mythical Icarus and was destroyed in the process.

Marlowe was a highly controversial figure as well as a glamorous, intelligent and sexually attractive one (see 'The Mysterious Death and Afterlife of Christopher Marlowe'). He made little secret of his blasphemous and atheistic views, relying on his Court connections to get him out of trouble if trouble arose. Among the utterances that would have got a lesser man into the Tower without delay were the two we met in the last story, which would have set the teeth on edge of any Elizabethan churchgoer, especially the Puritan ones: 'St John the Evangelist was bedfellow to Christ and leaned always in his bosom, that he used him as the sinners of Sodoma' and 'they that love not Tobacco & Boys are fooles'. Strong stuff, and not necessarily the views or the predilection of Thomas Kyd, despite the shared digs. It was customary, in an overcrowded city like the tiny hamlet that was the City of London then, for gentlemen to share lodgings; this by no means indicated that their relationship was sexual, or indeed that they were in any way more than friends.

Finally, the authorities had had enough of Marlowe's shenanigans and issued a warrant for his arrest. It had became increasingly obvious that he was deeply embroiled in the volatile and highly dangerous Elizabethan underground of spies and political intrigue, at the centre of which was the Queen's chief of intelligence, Sir Francis Walsingham.

11

Before Marlowe could be brought to justice, however, he was killed, stabbed with a dagger through the eye in a house in Deptford (not a tavern, as was put about at the time) on 30 May 1593.

Marlowe's rooms were the equivalent of an MI6 'safe house' and were searched before his death, making the official reason for his death – a fight over a bar bill – all the more implausible. Failing to find Marlowe (whose connections in any case were sufficient to get him off any minor charges), the authorities arrested his flatmate Thomas Kyd instead, and took him to Bridewell, the former palace of Henry VIII, which, in 1593, was used as a workhouse, orphanage and prison.

The prison, which in later years was to specialise in jailing and publicly flogging women, before they were eventually moved to the new prison at Holloway, had, in Elizabethan times, a notorious reputation for the torture of political prisoners. It was a low-profile Tower of London – away from the sort of publicity that incarceration in the Tower inevitably generated.

Kyd, under torture, insisted that the incriminatingly atheist pamphlets found by the soldiers sent to arrest Marlowe (and which may well have been planted in the rooms to incriminate him) were indeed Marlowe's. Having got an extra weapon in their campaign against him, Kyd was allowed to go.

However, he was now a broken man, physically and psychologically. He wrote one other play, *Cornelia*, in 1594, based on an existing French drama, but he died at the end of that year – penniless, and embittered. Marlowe had predeceased him by over a year, but that was no consolation to him. He had been fatally singed by his proximity to Marlowe's dangerous brilliance, a light that has continued to shine in the centuries since his death, while Kyd's has been eclipsed.

He deserves to be remembered, however, for his *Ur Hamlet*, which inspired arguably the greatest play ever written, and for his *The Spanish Tragedy*, which set the benchmark for revenge dramas by dozens of Elizabethan and Stuart dramatists, including Shakespeare himself. And, in a final irony, the place where this playwright in effect met his end is now a theatre near the site of the torture chamber where Kyd, who could in other circumstances have gone on to even greater things, was so cruelly treated.

AN ACTRESS WHO KNOWS WHAT SHE WANTS

PALL MALL, 1680

In a grand, newly built house, No. 79 Pall Mall, King Charles II entered the drawing room, with its fine view of gardens stretching down to nearby St James's Park – very close to his official residence, St James's Palace, and a short ride from his actual home at Whitehall. On his arm was Nell Gwynn, immortalised by Samuel Pepys, in his diaries, as 'Pretty, Witty Nell'. She was the King's favourite mistress, and an actress, though she had retired from the stage on taking up with the King. Indeed, it was the King's love for seeing an attractive actress on stage that revolutionised British theatre when the monarchy was restored in May 1660 and the long-cherished hope of the defeated cavaliers – that 'the King enjoys his own again' at last came true.

What Charles II enjoyed most was the company of attractive young women. When in exile in the Netherlands, he had often attended the theatre, and had doubly enjoyed it because, there, female parts were played by actresses – unlike the long-standing tradition in England that female roles be played by teenage boys. This had been a source of much fury in Puritan circles, who thought the theatre was quite corrupt enough without having boys in frocks on stage being wooed and variously raped, murdered or married. Having seized London when Civil War broke out, the Puritans soon ensured that all London playhouses were shut down, and Charles I's execution in 1649, and the creation of a republic under Cromwell, seemed to seal

14

the theatres' fate. However, against the odds, Charles II returned to power in 1660 and theatres were reopened under a Royal Charter – provided the female roles be actually played by women.

Nell's career had been one of the happiest results of this change of policy, and she had gone from being an orange seller in the intervals to a leading lady on the stage of the Theatre Royal, Drury Lane, where Pepys watched her with as much pleasure in her looks as her talent. That talent was primarily in light, comic roles, for she was indeed 'pretty, witty' and adept at judging the mood of an audience.

This was as true off stage as on. There was, for example, the occasion when, on her way to the theatre to watch a play, her coach was surrounded by a baying mob, who rocked it backwards and forwards, under the impression, because it was a suitably expensive coach, that it contained the Duchess of Portsmouth, another of the King's mistresses and one who happened to be Catholic – unpopular in those days. Nell pulled down the window of the carriage, stuck her head out so they could see whom they were really attacking, and shouted, 'Good people, you are mistaken! I am the Protestant whore!' At which their rage was turned to laughter and the carriage was allowed to proceed unmolested.

Now, in the house in Pall Mall, she was alone with an audience of one, but it was, as ever, the most important one she ever played to. And she knew exactly how to play him. Charles and Nell had arrived in the drawing room after a tour of the new house, and, before they got down to a different sort of business (in an upstairs room), the King finished his side of the transaction by presenting to Nell, with a suitable flourish, the deeds of the house.

Nell opened the document and read. The motto about not looking a gift horse in the mouth had flashed through her mind, but, for all her humour and charm, she was nothing if not businesslike. When she read that the house was to be given to her leasehold, she marched over to a nearby table, opened the inkpot and presented the King with a quill pen.

The famously black eyebrows shot up. 'What's the matter?

Does the house not suit?' Nell looked him straight in the eye. 'The house is given leasehold! I will accept nothing less than freehold. As Your Majesty well knows, I have always served freely under the Crown, and I expect a freehold in return!'

The King sighed, probably wondering whether she might not after all have been just as suited to playing Shakespeare's tragic heroines as she was the comic roles – and replaced the word 'leasehold' with 'freehold'. Which is why, to this very day, No. 79 Pall Mall is the only property in that part of St James's (still part of the Crown Estate) that is freehold rather than leasehold.

THE KING VERSUS THE PRINCE OF WALES

THEATRE ROYAL, DRURY LANE, LATE 1790s

It was an important night at Drury Lane. The Theatre Royal was expecting not one but two royal Georges – King George III and George, Prince of Wales. There was a certain nervousness of course, but the patronage of the two highest-ranking men in the kingdom would surely help keep the Theatre Royal's status as the smartest place to see and be seen in the capital.

As the King's carriage approached the theatre's entrance in Catherine Street (it was, then as now, the back of the theatre that adjoined Drury Lane), he was in a bad mood. He was tired of politics, still bitter over the loss of the American colonies some twenty years earlier – an event from which his temper never really recovered – and in a near-permanent state of fury at what was happening in France.

An ordered man who attached enormous significance to the proper way of doing things, to court etiquette and the importance of wearing the right clothes and medals, he had been – and still was – appalled at the French Revolution, which had broken out only a few years earlier.

The inexplicable way the gaggle of lower-class insurrectionists had held off the properly dressed and aristocratically led armies of the remaining European monarchies had enraged him even further – especially as in some respects it seemed a humiliating rerun of the American War of Independence, where a similar ragbag group of colonists had defeated the best troops the King could throw at them.

17

The carriage arrived at the theatre and the cavalry escort halted far enough from the carriage to let the people see their king, but near enough to stop them running up and assassinating him. Liveried grooms rushed to open the door. The theatre management were waiting, obsequiously. All seemed well.

The King emerged from the carriage, returned the escort's salute, graciously acknowledged the management's bows and entered the theatre foyer. He acknowledged the applause of those in the foyer, and felt himself beginning to relax.

Suddenly, there was a stir. The crowd was now looking over his shoulder, behind him. What could be going on? Was it an assassin? The King turned to look – and saw the hated figure of his eldest son, the Prince of Wales. There had been a tradition, throughout the eighteenth century, of kings and princes of Wales being at odds with each other, but never before had there been such a venomous level of ill feeling and mutual loathing as between this king and this prince.

'Good evening, Father,' said the Prince, bowing to the King in a way that managed to combine a casual approach with an exaggerated deference that suggested a complete contempt.

The King felt one of the red rages coming on – the inability to control himself that would, eventually, manifest itself not as rage but as madness, and leave the country in the hands of his detested son, as Prince Regent, for an entire decade before George finally died, after a sixty-year reign.

The rage took over. The King walked towards the Prince and, instead of a kiss on the cheek or a handshake, he curled his fingers into a fist and struck his son on the side of the head, sending him flying back onto the ground and at the feet of the group of friends and hangers-on who had accompanied him to the theatre.

The captain of the guard managed to prevent the King from further striking his son by the simple expedient of standing between them – ostensibly to protect the King from retaliation by the Prince, but actually to save the Prince further injury.

The theatre manager, appalled, ushered the King upstairs towards the royal box. As he did so, his mind was whirling:

Where would the Prince be seated? It was inconceivable to put him in the royal box with the King, yet what other box had the status appropriate to the Prince's station in life? And how were the two men to be kept apart at the interval, or leaving the theatre?

The problem was solved when the Prince chose to leave the theatre and find some other entertainment that night, but the management knew that the problem would not go away so easily.

They met the very next day to resolve the issue. Given that they were the Theatre Royal, they could not allow a repetition of the dreadful scene, nor could they afford to upset either the King or the Prince of Wales – who, judging by rumours about the King's mental health, might accede to power at any moment.

Finally an inspired – though expensive – decision was reached: to build two royal boxes, one for the King and one for the Prince, situated on either side of the stage (safely separated by one of the widest stages in Europe) and reached by separate grand staircases. Which is why, today, the Theatre Royal, Drury Lane, is the only theatre in England – indeed the world – with two separate royal boxes.

SHERIDAN'S FIRESIDE CHAT

DRURY LANE, 1809

No one was sure where this one started, but fires were very common in Regency London, and much feared. Buildings were made of wood and lit by candles and accidents were commonplace. So, when yet another building caught fire in Covent Garden, few would normally pay much attention.

But this wasn't just any building: it was the Theatre Royal, Drury Lane, and it had been constructed with the latest in Regency stage technology – a fire sprinkler system. Unfortunately, no one had bothered to put water into it.

The owner of Drury Lane was not far away. He was at the Houses of Parliament. His name was Richard Brinsley Sheridan, author of *She Stoops to Conquer* and *The Rivals* (among others) – the greatest comic playwright of his day.

But Sheridan had given up playwriting, profitable though it was, because he was determined to better himself socially, and so he went into politics as an MP, and sided with the Whigs. MPs were unpaid, so only gentlemen could afford to go into Parliament.

When news of the fire was brought to him Sheridan was on his feet making a speech. Demonstrating the stiff upper lip of the class he now belonged to, he insisted on finishing his speech, and only then did he make his way to Covent Garden.

The area, then as now, was full of wine bars, taverns and restaurants, and, as the theatre's would-be rescuers swarmed around the blazing building, Sheridan found a close-by tavern from which he could watch events unfold. He seated himself at an outside table with a flagon of wine in his hand, while his beloved Theatre Royal burned.

His friends remonstrated with him, Surely this was too upsetting to watch. Was his money not going up in smoke? At this point Sheridan showed some real class and, with his trademark humour, combining the wit that had made his fortune with the upper-class drawl that his friends employed. 'Not at all,' he said. 'Surely a man may take a glass of wine at his own fireside?'

EDMUND KEAN'S SHYLOCK

THEATRE ROYAL, DRURY LANE, 1814

The actor playing Shylock was sick with nerves. This was his first *Merchant of Venice* and he knew that if he got it wrong all London would soon learn of his failure. He was not very well known, although he had had some success in the title role of *Richard III*, but this was his big chance.

Shylock is a notoriously difficult part to negotiate. Shakespeare wrote him as a conniving, possessive, money-grabbing manipulator, a caricature of the worst Jewish stereotypes, and, while the 1800s were no more friendly to Jews than were Shakespeare's 1600s, he was a cartoon, almost suprahuman, and making him human was, and remains, a severe test of an actor. And yet Shakespeare's Jew is also a tragic figure, a brilliant and sensitive man twisted by years of abuse and anti-Semitism and leavened by his obsessive love for his daughter.

Puzzlingly, Shakespeare gives Shylock one of the great speeches about tolerance in all dramatic literature, an extraordinary peroration about the illogicality and evil of refusing to accept someone from a different race as being of equal value, as a fellow human – 'If you prick us, do we not bleed? If you tickle us do we not laugh?' – that makes him a remarkably eloquent and moving mouthpiece for humanity. The dilemma for an actor is to decide on the balance between all Shylock's conflicting characteristics.

So the man who was to play him this night at Drury Lane was afraid. This was his big chance, and he knew it. He felt sick

22

at the thought of failure, and even more sick at the fear of success and the inevitable pressure he would be under.

He started with a half-empty house: he was after all in effect an unknown. By the time the interval was over, word had spread. This was an extraordinary performance – more than that, it was clearly theatrical history in the making.

The box-office manager must have been pleasantly surprised as people came in from all over the West End, desperate to catch this amazing actor, and by the time he took his curtain call he was playing to a full house. In fact, the performance was a triumph and launched his career as a great tragic Shakespearean. This was the performance, Shylock at the Theatre Royal, Drury Lane, in January 1814, through which everything came good for him, and which opened the door to so many other, and grander, roles.

The actor shared the audience's elation, once saying that, when he was on form, it really was like flying – 'I could scarce feel the stage beneath me.' He turned out to be that one Shylock in every generation – it was Olivier in our own – who manages to bring everything together in one performance, and to convey the sheer power, the wickedness and the terror, the greed and the hurt, the love and the pain, of this towering figure, and his name was Edmund Kean.

Kean, born in 1787, had a very uneven career as an actor. He began as a child of four, playing Cupid in a ballet. His career wasn't helped by either his notoriously bad temper or his short stature (both of which must have helped him identify with one of his best-known roles, that of King Richard III), and Sarah Siddons, the great tragic actress, once dismissed him as 'that horrid little man'. But he was, from every account, a great actor.

This is a contemporary description of him as Shylock, as recorded by the critic and essayist William Hazlitt:

Mr Kean (of whom report had spoken highly) last night made his appearance at Drury-Lane Theatre in the character of Shylock. For voice, eye, action, and expression, no actor has come out for many years at all equal to him. The applause from the first scene to the last, was general, loud, and uninterrupted . . . by his admirable and expressive manner of giving the part [he] fully sustained the reputation he had acquired by his former representation of it, though he laboured under the disadvantage of considerable hoarseness.

He assumed a greater appearance of age and feebleness than on the first night, but the general merit of his playing was the same. His style of acting is, if we may use the expression, more significant, more pregnant with meaning, more varied and alive in every part, than any we have almost ever witnessed. The character never stands still; there is no vacant pause in the action; the eye is never silent. For depth and force of conception, we have seen actors whom we should prefer to Mr. Kean in Shylock; for brilliant and masterly execution, none.

Kean's private life (though married, he remained very much a ladies' man and was involved in a messy divorce case) excited the tabloids as much as his acting enthused theatregoers, and this eventually had an effect on his wider reputation. Two visits to America were artistic successes, each marred by terrible relations with the press, who were more interested in his morals as a man than his motivation as an actor.

Although his career went into a slump, he made the occasional attempted comeback and, appropriately, died (to all intents and purposes) on stage. On 25 March 1833 he was playing Othello to his son Charles's Iago in *Othello* at Covent Garden, more to satisfy his creditors than his famous love of the limelight. Before the curtain rose he had summoned his son to his dressing room, and told him, 'I am very ill, Charlie, I am afraid I shall be unable to act.'

This proved a prophecy. True, he was finally able to make it out of the wings and onto the stage with the encouragement of his son and the rest of the cast, but he was clearly ill. He was also drunk, having consumed 'for medicinal purposes' the bottle of spirits that had bedevilled his life almost as much as his love affairs, but, after the words 'Othello's occupation gone' (or 'Villain be sure', depending on whose conflicting account you prefer – all good theatre stories seem to have at least two versions), he collapsed into his son's arms. He just had the strength to say 'I am dying! Talk to them [the audience], Charles' before he fell into a coma from which he never recovered.

Kean was remembered for many roles, including Richard III, Othello, Iago and Macbeth, but it was Shylock that made him a star, thanks to his amazingly passionate, highly theatrical style that Coleridge once described – in one of the best accolades any actor has ever had, so we'll leave it with him – as 'like reading Shakespeare by flashes of lightning'.

THE GHOSTS OF DRURY LANE

LONDON, 1880s

Ask anyone who has appeared at the Theatre Royal, Drury Lane, if they know the Grey Man and they will at least have heard of him, if they have not had a personal relationship with him. He is one of several Drury Lane theatre ghosts who manifest themselves at irregular intervals to cast and backstage crew. Not in the least threatening, the Grey Man appears only during the day, not at night, when theatres can be pretty scary places.

His appearances are considered lucky, as they usually occur when the show in rehearsal is going to be a success. There haven't been any public accounts of the Grey Man's appearing to *The Producers*, nor was he seen during rehearsals for *Miss Saigon*, the theatre's longest-running musical, but he was seen by most of the cast of Ivor Novello's musical *The Dancing Years*. They were lined up on stage, ready for a cast photograph, when they saw him walking across the auditorium, wearing eighteenth-century clothes of a distinctly grey colour. *The Dancing Years* went on to be the most popular British musical of World War Two.

The Grey Man is a dapper figure in eighteenth-century dress who walks across the Dress Circle, from one side to another, before simply disappearing into the wall. For anyone to see him during rehearsals of a new show is taken as a very happy omen for that production.

Nobody knows exactly who he is, but he seems to have been the victim of a rather spectacular murder. In the course of the numerous restorations and adjustments to the fabric of the building that have been made over the last century or so, a 'false' wall was discovered at the spot in the auditorium where the Grey Man disappears, and was knocked down. Behind the wall, the building workers discovered the skeleton of a man, wearing eighteenth-century clothes, with a dagger in his ribs. And the Grey Man is by no means the only ghost who regularly haunts Drury Lane. There's also the Lilac Man.

There are those who think the Lilac Man is Dan Leno, probably the most popular music hall act in England in the 1880s, performing in up to twenty shows a night. His comic monologues were famous and he was even invited to entertain royalty at Sandringham, earning him the nickname, the Royal Jester. In 1896 he was hired by Augustus Harris, then manager at the Lane, to appear as the Dame in pantomime productions that included *Jack and the Beanstalk*, *Babes in the Wood* and *Mother Goose*. Not surprisingly, with this kind of schedule, he finally succumbed to a mental and physical breakdown and died in 1902.

Others attribute the ghost of the Lilac Man to a 'stage-door Johnny', one of the wealthy top-hatted men who called at the stage door after a musical to take one of the showgirls to dinner – and, he would hope, to bed.

Nobody knows why theatres have ghosts. Perhaps it's the intensity of the energy involved with putting on a play or a musical; perhaps it's the efforts of the actors and crew; perhaps the audience imbues the space with its own hopes and desires, but something in the air, in the walls, dressing rooms and even front of house, makes theatres so prone to the presence of ghosts.

Some of these are friendly, some are not, and the Dominion Theatre for one seems often to have some scary goings on, including strangely slamming doors and footsteps high in the flies above the stage, when the stage doorkeeper and the security man know that no one's there. Dogs, like cats and other animals, can often seem to pick on psychic phenomena that humans miss – they seem to operate on a different frequency. Which is why it can be so discomforting if you're sitting at home, alone with the cat, and your benign little tabby arches her back, sticks her tail straight up in the air, hisses at nothing and stares fixedly at something that, as far as you can see, isn't there.

One night at the Dominion, the noises were so insistent that the stage doorkeeper, believing there really was an intruder, called the police. They arrived quickly with their trained dogs. The police conducted an exhaustive search of the building and found nothing. Their dogs, though, went hysterical. Spooky.

HENRY IRVING AND ELLEN TERRY

LONDON, 1895

In 1895, Queen Victoria bestowed a knighthood on the actor Henry Irving. The whole of London society was scandalised. Since the Restoration, acting had been considered a job, not a profession, practised by raffish, somewhat unreliable persons of dubious character. The theatre was an enjoyable, though frankly disreputable, pursuit and those who attended the playhouses were dabbling in a slightly risqué undertaking, among people whose morals were, at best, suspect.

For an actor to be knighted, therefore, was a seismic change in the public perception. Overnight it went from being unthinkable to something that had received the Queen-Empress's seal of approval. As he rose having been tapped on the shoulders by Her Majesty's blade, Sir Henry Irving now represented the dignity of the acting profession.

The irony, of course, is that the actor who was so honoured actually did have suspect morals, by the standards of Victorian England in 1895. He may have been hopelessly old-fashioned, having spent some twenty years making the Lyceum Theatre the most impressive theatre in London, a centre of great Shakespearean productions and a powerhouse of the London stage, but he was also a ladies' man of some energy.

It might have stayed in his imagination were it not for his wife, Florence, a woman whose attitude towards the theatre was ludicrously snobbish even for a Victorian. More than twenty years before her husband received his knighthood, she was always urging this most successful of theatre managers and

29

most respectable of Shakespeareans to retire speedily from the stage, where he earned a very good living, and take an accountancy course instead. Even Florence acknowledged that he was a bit old to start a new career as an army officer and was in any case one of nature's gentlemen.

The final straw had come on the first night in 1871 – not long after he joined the Lyceum Theatre – of his biggest hit, *The Bells*. As he savoured his success on the journey home in their carriage, she enquired, 'Are you going to carry on making a fool of yourself all your life?'

Irving stopped the carriage, and, without another word, alighted. Florence continued with her journey home – and the rest of her life. He moved out of the matrimonial home that night, and, although he always invited her to each of his first nights, he was never to live with her again. She invariably accepted the private box and sat in it glowering at him across the auditorium but in their long lives they never spoke to each other again.

His amorous attentions were transferred to his Lyceum leading lady, Ellen Terry. While she was certainly not faithful to him, nor he to her, there was an undeniable bond between them and it lasted a lifetime. Office romances are hardly unknown, especially in the theatre, and theirs was to prove more durable than most.

OSCAR WILDE'S LAST FIRST NIGHT

ST JAMES'S THEATRE, 1895

The opening of his three-act comedy *The Importance of Being Earnest* at the St James's Theatre on Valentine's Day 1895, was both a public triumph and a private tragedy for Oscar Wilde. He had no way of knowing that this, the most successful evening of a magnificent career as a playwright, would be his last first night. Wilde was a highly intelligent man as well as a brilliantly funny one, but he had something of a death wish: an overintense interest in the Greek classics, perhaps.

Oscar's appearance belied his state of nerves. Described by one friend as having 'dressed with florid sobriety', he defiantly sported a green carnation – a known gay symbol – in his lapel. He knew that the evening would be far tenser than any normal first night. Not because author or actors were unsure of the quality of the play. Far from it. But because there was a very real chance that the evening would be disrupted – ruined – by an irate aristocrat, the Marquess of Queensberry.

Wilde knew, as the audience did not, that Queensberry was bent on his destruction. Queensberry – he of the Queensberry Rules in boxing – had already lost one son, his heir, Viscount Drumlanrig, in what was supposedly a shooting accident but was, in fact, a suicide. Queensberry and many others thought that Drumlanrig, who had worked for the Liberal prime minister, Lord Rosebery, had shot himself because he had had an affair with Rosebery that was about to be made public. Killing himself saved a public figure from disgrace. Queensberry was determined to save his other son, Lord Alfred

31

Douglas ('Bosie'), from a similar fate by making public the secret sexual affair between his son and Oscar Wilde.

The very idea that Douglas would shoot himself to save Wilde from a scandal is ludicrous. Douglas, a selfish young man who never thought of anyone's good but his own, goaded Wilde into taking action against his father – to sue him for criminal libel – after Queensberry had left a calling card at Wilde's club that accused him of 'posing as a *somdomite* [sic]'.

Now, as the ushers prepared to open the doors of the theatre to the public, Wilde fiddled with his cufflinks in nervous anticipation of what might happen. Sir George Alexander, the actor-manager, who was starring in *The Importance of Being Earnest*, had cancelled Queensberry's tickets and had arranged for police to be stationed at the front and rear of the theatre, to prevent a scene. This was a difficult enough task to accomplish, given that the police could not be told the exact nature of the feud that might lead an enraged marquess to attempt to storm a West End theatre.

As if to reflect the tempest going on between Queensberry and Wilde, there was a savage snowstorm that evening, but it was a mark of Wilde's popularity that London's most fashionable had all made the effort to attend, and there were no empty seats – other than those booked in Queensberry's name: Alexander decided not to rerelease them in case the marquess sent agents to cause a disturbance. In the event, there was no appearance from the crass and bullying marquess.

The curtain rose. The audience lapped up the comedy, the double lives led by the central characters (a coded comment on Wilde's own private life), and the wonderful one-liners so typical of their author. A huge success, the play received wonderful notices the next morning. However, the *New York Times* – which was not normally his greatest supporter, since aesthetes never went down very well in the States – was ironically mistaken in its praise: 'Oscar Wilde may be said to have at last, and with a single stroke, put his enemies under his feet.'

The opposite was of course the case. Wilde's libel case against Queensberry collapsed, and he was then tried for immoral behaviour and sentenced to two years' hard labour – the toughest sentence available to the judge for that particular crime.

Wilde's life had always been even more theatrical than his plays, and now it really had become something worthy of a Greek classic or of Shakespeare. The irony that his greatest theatrical triumph opened on a day dedicated to love was not lost on him. His fall appalled him, but even in the most ghastly circumstances he maintained the wit that had made him famous. Standing on a railway station platform, in fetters, while being transferred between prisons, he was recognised and spat at. His riposte was, 'If this is how Queen Victoria treats her prisoners, she doesn't deserve to have any!'

But the man who had delighted and shocked the society over which Victoria reigned had finally pushed that society too far. *The Importance of Being Earnest* closed in the light of Wilde's trial and sentence, and when it reopened his name was removed from posters – though eventually the pleasure that his plays gave the British public (however moral their own private lives) meant that his works, and his name, were resurrected.

By then, sadly, it was too late for the playwright, as he died in November 1900, in exile in Paris. Oscar Wilde's tragedy was that, despite his witty mockery of the British Establishment, as an artist he could operate only within the context of that establishment. Without it he had no audience (socially or professionally), could not earn any money and, denied a platform and the attire he required to perform on it, he became a broken man. Loss of liberty may have been a disgrace but it was the lack of a theatre that finished him off.

AN ACTOR DIES, A GHOST IS BORN

ADELPHI THEATRE, LONDON, 1897

The ghost of a handsome and immaculately turned-out man is often seen in Covent Garden, either in Maiden Lane or at the Covent Garden Tube station, on the corner of James Street and Long Acre. The man was a leading actor named William Terriss, who has been dead since 1897.

Maiden Lane is a small, quaint little road that parallels the Strand and it contains London's oldest restaurant, Rules, a Catholic church, several olde-worlde little alleys that run between it and the Strand, and not one but two stage doors. One leads to the small Vaudeville Theatre, the other to the much larger Adelphi, now displaced slightly to the right of where it used to be. It is at the site of the Adelphi's original stage door that the ghost of the elegant Victorian gentleman regularly appears.

William Terriss was a matinée idol of Victorian London who, after an early start trying out a wide range of jobs, finally settled on that of an actor. Helped by his striking good looks, he was soon a popular performer, playing romantic leads and men of action. He acted for some time in the theatre company of Victorian Britain's leading actor (and first knight – see 'Henry Irving and Ellen Terry') Sir Henry Irving, but found his true home at the Adelphi, a theatre specialising in melodramas.

At fifty he was handsome, successful, at the peak of his fame. His beautiful daughter, Ellaline, had recently married another successful actor and theatre owner, Seymour Hicks. But, sadly, as Terriss approached the Adelphi stage door on 16 December

1897, his fate awaited him in the shape of a deranged and unemployed actor called Richard Arthur Prince. Convinced, entirely wrongly, that Terriss had ruined his life, Prince lunged at him with a knife and fatally stabbed him in a crazed attack.

Prince did quite well out of the murder, for although he was arrested, tried and sentenced to life imprisonment in a secure mental hospital, he happily passed the years organising the other inmates in theatrical entertainments.

Not long after Terriss's death, reports came of seeing his ghost striding towards the stage door, as if determined, this time, actually to enter the theatre. He has been seen in the area ever since.

Did he have a fascination for the then new underground train service? No, he had a sweet tooth and often, on his way to the theatre, he used to buy pastries and cakes from a baker whose shop was by the side of the station entrance. His ghost, only one of many theatrical apparitions in Covent Garden, apparently still enjoys the pleasurable memories that the site holds for it. Nice to know that, even in the afterlife, there's a place for comfort food.

BEERBOHM TREE'S WANDERING EYE

HER MAJESTY'S THEATRE, EARLY 1900s

Herbert Beerbohm Tree was one of the giants of the Victorian and Edwardian theatre, a brilliant actor and manager whose greatest achievement (of many) was the building in 1897 and subsequent management of Her Majesty's Theatre in London's Haymarket. His productions were lavish dramas, full of spectacular sets and clever stage technology that allowed for quick and dramatic scene changes. He was knighted for services to the theatre in 1909.

Tree was a half-brother of the writer and theatre critic Max Beerbohm, and no mean wit himself, his own sense of humour manifesting itself in one-liners worthy of the best of Oscar Wilde's aphorisms. When directing an assortment of actresses in a scene in which they were meant to be pure and demure, he overheard them swearing as they lined up and enjoined them, 'Ladies! Ladies! Just a *little* more virginity, if you don't mind!'

With a critic for a brother, he was always aware of the adversarial relationship between critics and practitioners and was not above taking the occasional swipe at his tormentors. Speaking of a pretentious theatre critic who liked to season his reviews with Latin and Greek phrases, he said, 'He's a whippersnapper of criticism who uses dead languages to hide his ignorance of life.' He didn't hesitate to poke fun at himself, either, and, although proud of his own reputation as a performer, he commented, 'When I pass my name in such large letters I blush, but at the same time instinctively raise my hat!'

In 1883 Tree married the comic actress Helen Maud Holt, who often played opposite him, and from all accounts it was a happy and successful marriage that lasted – in spite of some extramarital adventures – until his death. They lived in a private apartment on the top of Her Majesty's Theatre and were very proud of the décor of both theatre and private rooms. Tree was very un-Victorian in his preference for simplicity in furnishings: 'The national sport of England is obstacle-racing. People fill their rooms with useless and cumbersome furniture, and spend the rest of their lives in trying to dodge it.'

But as he got older his eye started to wander, and he had plenty of opportunities to indulge his interest in partners who were younger than his long-suffering wife. He was, after all, an honoured member of a profession where he had a high profile, he was admired, he was rich, and through his work was constantly meeting aspiring new members of the business.

There's nothing unusual in this, of course, but where Tree rather bucked the trend was that, despite being something of a ladies' man when he was young, in later life his tastes ran increasingly towards young men. Though, it has to be said, his interest was far more discreetly expressed than that other late Victorian theatrical giant, Oscar Wilde (see 'Oscar Wilde's Last First Night'), and was also safely confined, in general, to young actors who would stand to lose everything should they try to blackmail him – unlike the rent boys and assorted working class lads that Oscar Wilde and Lord Alfred Douglas used to enjoy.

Helen, his wife, was a fine actress with intelligence and a sense of humour. While she appreciated the convenience of 'living above the store', she recognised also that it gave her wandering husband a perfect venue to pursue his extracurricular love interests.

On one such occasion, on a warm summer's evening at the height of the Edwardian era, when Tree was heading for his knighthood and all seemed well with his world, he had a beautiful young actor to dinner at his theatre flat. Along, of course, with his wife, for proprieties had to be observed – especially after what had happened to Oscar Wilde.

Mrs Beerbohm Tree made polite conversation – which

wasn't difficult, as the boy was charming – with her husband and his guest. Eventually, after dessert, it was time, as at all well-mannered Edwardian dining tables, for the ladies – or in this case the lady – to withdraw while the gentlemen enjoyed their cigars, brandy and rather racier conversation than they had dared earlier in the evening.

As she went to the dining room door, Mrs Beerbohm Tree turned, looked at the two men, who she knew would be in each other's arms the moment she left the room, then looked, pointedly, at the conveniently placed chaise longue, where the inevitable seduction would be facilitated. (Not for nothing had Mrs Patrick Campbell, an Edwardian actress and beauty, referred to marriage as 'Ah, the deep, deep peace of the double bed after the hurly burly of the chaise longue!')

Turning her cool, direct gaze on the two men again, she nodded to the boy then said, over her shoulder as she left the room, 'Good night, Herbert. And remember, it's adultery all the same!'

Sir Herbert Beerbohm Tree died of a thrombosis after an operation on his knee, in 1917. Lady Tree died in 1937, after another twenty years of life and theatregoing. Her Majesty's, Tree's greatest monument, is still standing, and has for nearly twenty years been the home to Andrew Lloyd Webber's *The Phantom of the Opera*. Whether Tree's phantom still haunts the site of his old rooms has not been established, but, if he does, and is accompanied by the spirits of any of his many conquests, we can be sure that Lady Tree's ghost is also hovering somewhere in the background, delivering coolly elegant one-liners before she discreetly leaves them to do whatever it is ghostly lovers do.

OPENING THE COLISEUM: TWO TECHNICAL DISASTERS

LONDON COLISEUM, 1904

The newly restored London Coliseum, the present home of English National Opera and Ballet, reopened for business in 2004 after a multimillion-pound refurbishment, in time to mark the centenary of its first opening in 1904.

Of all the designs of the theatre architect, the matchless Frank Matcham, the 1904 London Coliseum was the grandest. It was meant to be. Sir Oswald Stoll, one of the era's greatest impresarios, ordered it as his flagship playhouse, and it cost him the staggering sum of £300,000. Located in St Martin's Lane, just north of Trafalgar Square and the landmark St Martin-in-the-Fields, the Coliseum was, as its name implies, intended to conjure up 'the grandeur that was Rome'. Just as importantly to Matcham and Stoll, it was to showcase the very latest in British stage technology. An oxymoron, you might think. And you'd be right. As so often happens, the idea was right; where it fell down was in its execution.

Matcham designed many revolutionary features for the Coliseum stage, including a dazzling triple revolve. This meant that the variety acts that gave the theatre its life could be changed, with all the requisite props and scenery, very rapidly. The revolves were so large that the upcoming acts could be set up while the onstage act was performing, ready to be literally turned round without the audience having to wait through a tiresome scene change.

Unfortunately (and for Brits this has a truly depressing inevitability about it), in that first all-important week, the technology went wrong – on two separate occasions.

Poor Sir Oswald had already had to deal with the usual teething troubles, not least that there was a 'pea-souper' of fogs on the originally planned opening night, 19 December. One of those notorious London fogs that seem so romantic now, and look great in old movies about mystery and murder in Victorian London, had descended. It was of course hugely inconvenient, not to say murderous for anyone with asthma, and so the opening of the Coliseum had to be delayed until Christmas Eve, 24 December 1904. That was rather too close to Christmas Day for comfort, of course, but it was the only available day for the guest of honour, so the 24th it had to be.

Stoll and his subordinates at the Coliseum were delighted that their magnificent theatre was to be opened by the King himself, Edward VII, accompanied by his famously beautiful consort, Queen Alexandra. Edward VII was a hugely impressive-looking man, his vast girth (not for nothing was he nicknamed 'Tum Tum') and manly beard giving him an appropriately regal, and engagingly worldly, look. True, he was so large that he could never do up his lowest waistcoat button – which is why it became, and has remained, the fashion for no gentleman ever to do up the lowest button of his own waistcoat – but this simply added to the stateliness of his personage.

This size and the, er, stateliness (not unknown to me and other members of my family) made Stoll ask the incomparable Frank Matcham to allow, in his building plans, for a sort of movable royal box. This was designed to be not unlike a railway carriage, though much larger and more opulent, and was designed to carry the royals, with no visible effort, and saving Edward's legs, directly to their seats. It fitted into the front of the Coliseum, on St Martin's Lane (the lower classes had a separate entrance in the courtyard at the side) and moved, graciously and gently, along its own little set of rails, through the foyer and into the back of the proper royal box, located at the rear of the stalls and with a fabulous view.

The King and Queen duly arrived in St Martin's Lane, having travelled the relatively short distance from Buckingham Palace (only ten or fifteen minutes' trot along the Mall and round Trafalgar Square), accompanied by a detachment of cavalry and mounted police.

They were greeted, with much bowing and curtseying, and all due ceremony, and were graciously pleased, as the Court Circular always put it, to step into the mobile royal box, ready to glide regally to their seats.

So far, so good, and the souvenir programme printed for the occasion explained what would happen next:

Immediately upon entering the Theatre, the Royal party will step into a richly furnished lounge, which, at a signal, will move softly along a track formed in the floor, through a salon into a large foyer, which contains the entrance to the Royal Box. The Lounge-Car remains in position at the entrance to the Box and serves as an ante-room during the performance.

Unfortunately – and wouldn't you know it? – the box juddered briefly, then came to a grinding halt. Sweat poured down the face of the box's operator, wearing a stiff starched shirt collar that his neck certainly wasn't used to, and that merely added to his considerable discomfort. Stoll's face took on a look like thunder, and he dared not look at the King, who, like many of his relatives, had a ferocious temper. Even the mild-mannered King George VI, the present Queen's father and Edward's grandson, was to be famous in family circles for his 'gnashes' – explosions of rage that only his wife could control.

Happily for Stoll, the King was on this occasion inclined to see the funny side of it. Or maybe it was that losing his temper in public would look bad-mannered and in any case appear rather impotent – there's no point in throwing a wobbly unless it gets results, and if the 'car' wasn't going to work in any case he would have looked foolish. Inconceivable. So he did the most appropriate thing – which was to burst into laughter. This made him look genial as well as regal, and as he set off the short distance to the royal box on foot, earned him a spontaneous round of applause from onlookers.

While embarrassing, the incident was hardly disastrous – it's only about 30 feet from the street to the royal box – and the rest of the evening was a sufficient success that Sir Oswald Stoll's pride was restored. Eugene Stratton topped the Coliseum's first bill with his act as 'The Whistling Coon', fully blacked up. His greatest hit was to come seven years later, in 1911, with 'The Lily of Laguna', but he was already a major draw and from all accounts the King loved his act.

A week later, however, came a real tragedy. In an effort to show off the triple revolve to best advantage, Stoll overreached himself by deciding to stage a spectacle nothing less than the Derby. The Derby was then, as now, an enormously popular race, and a favourite of the King. When he was Prince of Wales his horses had won two Derbys, and he was to win another in 1909, when he was King. Maintaining his luck on the racecourse to the end, he was to hear, on his deathbed on 6 May 1910, that his horse, Witch of the Air, had won at Kempton Park.

Stoll therefore thought a horse race, on stage, using the fast-moving revolves, would be a good idea. This is not as odd as it sounds for a variety theatre in which anything and everything that could be defined as 'entertainment' was welcome. There was a long tradition of using animals on stage in London. The Theatre Royal, Drury Lane, will to this day show you the backstage pens where elephants used to be kept and no epic Shakespeare or operatic spectacular was complete without horses.

The RSPCA would probably baulk at staging horse races on stage today, but in 1904 at the new London Coliseum, the Derby seemed a good idea at the time. The race, of course, was a disaster waiting to happen.

One of the horses involved slipped/skidded/was hurled by the moving revolve off the stage, and into the orchestra pit, killing the jockey and injuring several musicians.

And that is why, in every theatre with an orchestra pit, you can today see safety nets or grids between the stage and the audience, covering part of the pit, and why the one at the Coliseum is so much wider than most.

Incidentally, the innovative mobile royal box was never made to work, but that hasn't stopped successive members of the royal family crossing that 30 feet on foot to enjoy whatever the Coli has to offer.

THE FIRST PETER PAN

DUKE OF YORK'S THEATRE, 1904

Peter Pan seems to have been with us for ever, but the character was actually born on 27 December 1904, not perhaps in a trunk but certainly in a theatre. True, he had already appeared in a book, *The Little White Bird*, in 1902, but that was more a premonition than an arrival. It was with the play that he took the form we all know as 'the boy who wouldn't grow up'.

Peter's creator, J M (James) Barrie, was a brilliant playwright whose wider work (especially *Dear Brutus*, a study of whether or not we really could change our lives if we had that longed-for second chance) is not as well known as it should be. This is largely Peter's fault because it is on Peter's elfin head and escapades that Barrie's immortality rests.

But the story of how the play came into being, and of its first-night success, is, in some ways, stranger than anything Peter may have told Wendy.

Barrie was a strange, quirky man of great intelligence and a complicated private life: his elder brother David had died, aged 13, when Barrie was a child, and the shock had more or less unhinged their mother. James Barrie tried to act, talk and even dress like his deceased brother, to convince her that her older son was still alive.

As an adult, Barrie, possibly as a result of spending his own childhood pretending to be a ghost who never grew up, proved to be asexual, his marriage to an actress, not surprisingly, ending in divorce. They had no children, just a large dog that was not so much a child substitute as company for Barrie on his

44

long walks in the park. On one of these solitary walks in Kensington Gardens, he met the five sons of a barrister, Arthur Llewelyn Davies, and his wife, Sylvia.

Although a full-grown adult, Barrie was psychologically more boy than man and it was as a boy that he befriended the children. They took an immediate shine to him, especially when he began to make up stories to amuse them. These stories were, of course, the adventures of Peter Pan.

Peter Pan grew out of his many chats and storytelling sessions with the boys, but it reflects a major and very dark theme of his life and work – his inability to deal with his own adult emotions and sexuality, his belief that life after the age of twelve didn't amount to all that much, and that death was almost to be welcomed as a reprieve for the sorrows of living – 'To die will be an awfully big adventure.'

While all this gives psychologists plenty of speculative material, what is most important about *Peter Pan* is that it gave its readers and audiences a perennially fascinating and wonderfully imaginative adventure story with pirates, Red Indians, magic flying powers, fairies, a lost land and the chance to escape parental control – by literally flying out of the window and off to another world.

This heady combination so excited the producer Charles Frohman on first reading that he commissioned a stage version immediately. He was so taken with the script that he would stop friends in the street and act out little parts of it. He had already decided that the part of Peter would be played in New York by an actress, Maude Adams, and in London, by Nina Boucicault. Its success, he knew, was without question.

The rehearsals (which began towards the end of October 1904) were shrouded in secrecy, ostensibly to keep the plot a surprise, but one can't help thinking that it might also have been to stir up interest in the play – everyone (especially the press) likes a secret.

Even the cast were given only the pages they really needed for rehearsals, and it came as a shock to them to hear that they would be flying on stage: Hilda Trevelyan, the actress playing Wendy, was understandably rather shaken when she turned up at the stage door of the Duke of York's Theatre to be told she couldn't start rehearsals until she had proved to the management that her life had been properly insured.

Perhaps the most important casting was that of Captain Hook, who was to be played by Gerald Du Maurier. Du Maurier was not only a leading actor-manager of Edwardian London, but happened to be Sylvia Llewelyn Davies's brother as well. He decided to play not just Hook but Mr Darling too, pointing up yet another Freudian subplot in the play: a father as a terrifying authority figure who must be successfully defeated if his children are to be able to grow into adults themselves.

As with many of the best stage successes, things had gone wildly wrong through the later stages of rehearsals and up to the actual day of the premiere itself. At one point, recalled Barrie years later, 'A man dressed in overalls, carrying a mug of tea or a paint box, used often to appear by my side in the shadowy stalls and say to me, "The Gallery boys won't stand it." He then mysteriously faded away as if he were the theatre ghost.'

As the original opening date (22 December) approached, things went from bad to worse, with a large part of the set being smashed when a mechanical lift collapsed. Barrie suffered from nervous exhaustion and stress-induced migraines, and it was decided to postpone opening until the 27th. He made a huge number of last-minute changes in the script, which drove the poor cast to distraction as they had to learn new dialogue several times a day. But still he continued writing and rewriting, all through Christmas, which for the company was very much a working day, although the scene painters refused to work over the holiday.

So worried was Barrie about the potential lack of audience response (and, after all, audience response was hardly a normal part of Edwardian West End theatregoing) that he had arranged – in the event of the appeal to clap 'if you believe in fairies' being met by resounding silence – for the orchestra to give a round of applause from the depths of the orchestra pit. He also arranged for Gerald Du Maurier to give impersonations of Sir Henry Irving (the famous Victorian actor-manager – see 'Henry Irving and Ellen Terry') in front of the stage curtain if the scene changes (which were maddeningly slow in rehearsal) took too long!

He need not have worried. The audience was charmed, amused, entertained and engrossed from the moment the play began, and when Nina Boucicault asked them if they believed in fairies they responded so loudly and enthusiastically that she burst into tears. The critics loved it – *The Times* thought that '*Peter Pan* is from beginning to end a thing of pure delight' and most others agreed, except for a rather bitter George Bernard Shaw who felt that it was 'foisted on children by grown-ups', and the writer Anthony Hope (*The Prisoner of Zenda*) more amusingly sighed after an evening watching the Lost Boys of Neverland, 'Oh, for an hour of Herod!'

The play was a triumph, and certainly not just with the adults. Gerald's daughter, Daphne Du Maurier, wrote, in a book about her father and his part in *Peter Pan*:

> When Hook first paced his quarter-deck in the year of 1904, children were carried screaming from the stalls . . . How he was hated, with his flourish, his poses, his dreaded diabolical smile! That ashen face, those blood-red lips, the long, dank, greasy curls; the sardonic laugh, the maniacal scream, the appalling courtesy of his gestures . . .

Hook has remained in many ways the most intriguing character, certainly more easily identified with – or against – than the far more mysterious Peter Pan, who is, these days, more often played by a young man than the traditional cross-dressing actress.

The play, for all its dark side, is nonetheless great fun and Peter's sexual and emotional development has given rise to many offstage anecdotes. Once, when the late writer and broadcaster Arthur Marshall was in the audience at a later production of *Peter Pan* when my grandmother Gladys Cooper was playing Peter, he recalled the moment in the play when Wendy asks how old Peter is. At that point a small child, with a voice and a worldliness more suited to a cavalry officer than a schoolboy, drawled, 'About thirty-five, I should say!'

47

Barrie's extraordinary interest in and great affection for the Llewelyn Davies brothers continued until his death. Indeed, when both parents died in their mid-forties, within a few years of each other, Arthur in 1907, Sylvia in 1910, they trusted their most precious possessions, their five sons, to James Barrie, 'leaving' them to him in Sylvia's will, and he remained their guardian until they reached their majority. Their relationship has raised eyebrows, but the boys themselves, though sometimes ambivalent about his emotional closeness to them, were always adamant that there was never the slightest hint of anything improper or untoward in his behaviour.

Two of the boys subsequently committed suicide – Michael in 1921, in a gay suicide pact with a fellow student (they tied their hands together and drowned), while Peter threw himself under a tube train at Sloane Square underground station in 1960. George perished in Flanders in 1915, one of the millions of casualties of World War One. Jack lived until 1959, and Nico, the youngest, to 1980.

And in Kensington Gardens, where they met and started the relationship that proved so valuable and life-defining to them all, there is now a statue of Peter Pan.

THE KAISER MAKES A THEATRICAL JOKE

BERLIN, 1917

It was July 1917, three years into World War One. A few months earlier, in March, the Russian monarchy had been overthrown, and the Tsar and his family imprisoned in their palace at Tsarskoe Selo, a few miles outside St Petersburg. With anti-German feeling running high in Russia as a result of the war, the fact that the Empress, Alexandra, had been a German princess was a major reason for the unpopularity of the royal family. Throughout the war she had been sneered at as 'the German spy', and despite the Tsar's renaming of St Petersburg with the more Russian name of Petrograd in 1915, his dynasty was on the rocks. His wife's family, on the other hand, was flourishing.

All the European royals were closely related and the German royal family, led by Kaiser Wilhelm, dearly loved both the Empress of Russia and her sister, Elizabeth (now married to a Russian Grand Duke), and had been close to them when they were still German princesses in the 1880s and 1890s, before their marriages.

Kaiser Wilhelm, who saw war as a matter of chivalry, was astonished that he had been stripped of his honorary regimental titles in the British Army, and that his banner, as a knight of the Garter, had been removed from the ceiling of St George's chapel, Windsor. He was not known for a great sense of hilarity – his was a coarse sense of humour, and when he did laugh, it was usually at other people's expense. Yet a momentous change in the British royal family produced the one and only joke for which he is known. And it was a theatrical, indeed a Shakespearean, joke at that.

The Kaiser was half English – his father was heir to the throne of Prussia (and then Germany) and his mother was Victoria, the eldest daughter of Queen Victoria – which explained his love–hate relationship with England, his exasperating but affectionate relationship with his grandmother, Queen Victoria (who died in his arms at Osborne), and his knowledge of English theatre.

On a July morning in 1917, an *aide de camp* approached the Kaiser's desk, clicked his heels and gave him the daily newspaper. There on the front page was the announcement, by King George V of England – whose wife, Queen Mary, had been born a German princess (Princess May of Teck) – that from now on the royal family's name was changed from Saxe-Coburg-Gotha to Windsor.

Alarmed by the virulent anti-German feeling in Britain, shocked at the fall of the Russian monarchy, and determined to keep his own throne, King George V had decided to make a clean break with the family's partly German past and thus insulate himself – and especially his wife – from any possible revolutionary activity.

This seemed to the Kaiser both cowardly and ludicrous. He summoned his wife, the Empress Augusta Victoria, and read her the details. 'What will you do?' she asked. 'I propose', replied the Kaiser, twirling his magnificent moustache, which was specially waxed every day to bestow its dramatic shape, 'to take the entire family to the theatre, to see a production of *The Merry Wives of Saxe-Coburg-Gotha!*'

LADY DIANA COOPER IN 'THE MIRACLE'

BROADWAY, 1923

Lady Diana Manners was a glacially beautiful aristocrat who was a treasured member of the Prince of Wales's social set in the 1920s and 1930s. She and her husband, Duff Cooper (later Viscount Norwich) were close to the Prince and were regular guests at his beloved country home, Fort Belvedere, near Windsor Castle.

After World War One, Cooper was appointed ambassador to France, and, as Lady Diana Cooper, his wife was to be as successful a hostess and centre of literary and artistic Paris as she had been in England.

Before the war she had been courted by some strikingly attractive, well-connected and wealthy young men – including Raymond Asquith, Patrick Shaw-Stewart, Edward Horner, Duff Cooper and Sir Denis Anson. But the war, which claimed an entire generation of young men, took all but one of her suitors, leaving the last (and her favourite), Duff Cooper, to claim her as his prize.

Though very bright, Cooper had little money of his own and, given their expensive tastes and the fact that Diana was a duke's daughter, money was essential. The Duke of Rutland acknowledged her as his daughter but his Duchess had had a well-known affair with a dashingly handsome Victorian adulterer called Harry Cust and it was generally believed in society circles that he was, in fact, her father.

When they married, Diana hoped that her startlingly good

51

looks might earn them some money – and so it proved. She belonged to the first generation of working society figures, and she wanted to make her own mark on the world rather than just be the friend and confidante of London's Bright Young Things. One of those movers and shakers, Evelyn Waugh, was later to immortalise her in his novels as Mrs Stitch, a society woman who has writers and newspaper editors equally at her feet.

She found her artistic moment in 1924, in New York, when she created her own Madonna mania, playing a statue of the Virgin Mary that comes to life in Max Reinhardt's *The Miracle*. This play-cum-ballet-cum-pageant-cum-panto had been a success before World War One at the *Deutschesteater* in Germany. Reinhardt now wanted to revive it for a new generation, and needed someone of extraordinary physical grace to play the Madonna. Who better than an English aristocrat whose chiselled beauty and flawless complexion made her one of the most famous beauties in Europe? His request to meet her, in the summer of 1923, came at the perfect time for Diana and Duff.

The Miracle concerns a young nun led astray by an enticingly wicked man who persuades her to run away with him. In order to cover up the nun's absence from the convent, the statue of the Virgin Mary, before whom she prays every day in happier, calmer times, steps down from her niche in the convent wall to take on the nun's duties. The nun, thus replaced and therefore not missed, returns with her dead baby (it has been an eventful time in the outside world) who is then miraculously transformed into the Christ child and takes its place in the Madonna's arms.

This may all sound too much to bear but, when done well, it was surprisingly effective, and required very little actual acting for Diana. Almost all she had to do was to stand around looking beautiful and serene. Perfect. She accepted the part with alacrity and set sail for New York, where she arrived to a carefully orchestrated storm of publicity as to whether or not Diana or the original Madonna, Maria Carmi, would play the role on opening night. Reinhardt decided to share the role between them after La Carmi, who had starred in *The Miracle* in 1912, had threatened to sue: 'It is my life. Without me *The Miracle* would fail. It is fate.'

Diana was unused to these perfectly commonplace American shenanigans and was secretly thrilled to find herself at the centre of a major theatrical row, especially when she discovered that the drawing of lots to see who would play on opening night was rigged to ensure that she won.

The rest of the cast were less enthusiastic about a star who was not only an amateur but a titled foreign one at that, but Reinhardt, who had come over to New York to watch the rehearsals and see the show open, was delighted with Diana's performance. The first night was nerve-racking for Diana but a triumph for the production, which was greeted with a fifteen-minute ovation and rave notices. The combination of reviews and public interest in Diana herself drew capacity audiences, and Diana added to her reputation by playing the part of the nun on the evenings when the Madonna was played by Maria Carmi. She enjoyed both roles but looked the more striking as the Madonna.

Sixty years before a more widespread Diana-mania, New York was gripped with admiration for a Lady Diana fever of its own. When the New York season closed, in June 1924, the entire company collected together outside the theatre to cheer her as she left for England.

For a further three years she was to tour with the play, an experience she appreciated for the combination of adoration and ready cash, but as with all tours it had its own trials. On one occasion a fly landed on her face and, playing a statue, she had to put up with it while remaining motionless. Then there was the time when a pair of starstruck Siamese twins came to see the play. Perhaps hoping for a miracle of their own, they sat, joined at the back, watching sideways as the action unfolded on the stage. Unfortunately, the audience were more interested in them than the play, and the cast, too, as soon as the curtain call was over, peeked from behind the curtain to see the twins get up from their seats and shuffle off towards the exit.

The Miracle was not just an American hit: it came to Europe, too, appearing, among other places, at the Salzburg Festival in

1925. The burst of European culture was refreshing for Diana, who was growing a little tired of the United States, and especially of Los Angeles, whose people she described as common, badly dressed and dull. 'All the women are blowzy blondes . . .' But there was a consolation, in that she got to meet John Gilbert, the silent-movie star now chiefly remembered as Greta Garbo's lover.

Back in Europe in 1927 she embarked with *The Miracle* on another tour, this one ending in Vienna. It was a stellar cast that included Leonid Massine, the ballet star, as the man who leads the nun astray, Glen Byam Shaw and Tilly Losch, the Austrian dancer and actress, as the nun. Miss Losch was a practical joker and she sewed up the head opening of her nun's habit so that Diana as the Madonna statue, ended up flailing about wildly, trying to find the gap where she would normally insert her head, instead of slipping into the habit and emerging with her customary grace.

George V, never a great theatre expert, was typically bluff – and insensitive – when he came round backstage to see her after one performance: 'Does it not tire you to stand so long with your head on one side?' 'Yes, sir, it is a little tiring.' 'Still, you don't have any words to say, and that's three-quarters of what acting is about!'

After a three-month run at the Lyceum in London, Diana decided that she would – to the horror of her many aristocratic friends – like to tour the provinces, so she duly took *The Miracle* round the country, calling at, among other dates, Liverpool Manchester, Glasgow and Southampton.

It was during this tour that she met and became friends with Evelyn Waugh, a friendship that was to be punctuated with furious rows but one that, ultimately, was a source of great pleasure to both of them. For Waugh, who was to become Britain's most famous Roman Catholic novelist, part of the attraction must have been, if only subconsciously, being best friends with the Madonna.

Another of her friends was Noël Coward, whom she upset after she had been to see his great patriotic pageant *Cavalcade* at the Theatre Royal, Drury Lane, in 1931. *Cavalcade* was not at all like his other plays, brittle and funny, and at a dinner party some time later she said to Coward, 'Oh, Noël, I did so enjoy seeing *Cavalcade*! I simply laughed and laughed!' To which Coward acidly replied, 'And I was thrilled to see you in *The Miracle*. I couldn't stop laughing all through it!'

The last performance of Diana's *The Miracle* came, prosaically, at the Hippodrome, Golders Green, at the end of January 1933. From now on she would concentrate on being the hostess wife, aiding Duff's career.

She and Duff continued to be part of the Prince of Wales's circle, and were among his closest friends when he became King Edward VIII. After Edward's abdication in December 1936, many people thought that the Coopers would be excluded from the new court, but early in 1937 they were invited to 'dine and sleep' at Windsor Castle, and were clearly back in favour.

She lived for another half a century, long enough to see the rise of another Lady Diana – Diana Spencer, later Princess of Wales, and to see the emergence of a superstar called Madonna. As she continued her progress through the smarter – and more artistic – London social circles until her death in 1986, it must have amused her to think of how she had combined those two roles, Diana and Madonna, in theatres on both sides of the Atlantic, all those years ago.

THE WEST END'S WORST FIRST NIGHT?

DALY'S THEATRE, 1927

Talk to any American theatregoer about going to the theatre in London and he or she will tell you how well the British behave. None of the vulgar applause in inappropriate places so common on Broadway, they say, no standing ovations for the scenery. No, the British behave impeccably in the theatre, always have. Well, no. Not in fact.

Failure brings out the worst in everyone and everyone enjoys the *schadenfreude* of theatrical disaster. Perhaps the worst ever opening night belonged to two men with whom the word 'failure' was almost never associated, which is what makes this story strange. These days, as Noël Coward revivals follow one after the other, like the seagulls he would count while resting on the cruise liners on which he would frequently 'sail away' for some much-needed rest, it seems impossible to think of Coward – especially his younger self – as a failure. But it was a play of his that was perhaps the most famously, gloriously disastrous first night in twentieth-century British theatre and whose title ever afterwards became the adjective given to theatrical flops.

The play was called *Sirocco*, appropriately named, you might think, for those inexplicable Mediterranean hot winds that blow up suddenly and devastate the landscape in a short sharp burst. It was set in Italy, the story of a hot-blooded young testosterone-laden Italian waiter who falls for – and eventually turns nasty and beats up – an English Rose, a tourist on holiday.

It called for a leading man who was demonstrably macho, a Mediterranean Lothario who could overwhelm and seduce a suggestible young woman with one or two practised come-hither glances. Noël's first choice for the role was the fey and frankly effeminate star, now better remembered as the composer and playwright of romantic musicals, and Noël's best rival and friend, Ivor Novello.

He sent the script to Novello, who promptly turned it down. Ivor, despite the odd mistake, was basically a very good judge of scripts, and knew instinctively that *Sirocco* was a stinker and, in any case, not for him. But Noël, only three years after his first great success, *The Vortex*, had the invincibility of the very young – he was only 26 and a big star – and was convinced that the play would be a big hit if only he could persuade Ivor to play in it. Ivor said no. His Welsh practicality and good theatrical instincts told him it wasn't going to work.

Many dinners at the Ivy followed. Noël used all his famous powers of persuasion on his friend. And, he wheedled, hadn't *The Vortex* been a horror story, financially and artistically, right up until opening night? Hadn't it required an embarrassing though ultimately fruitful lunch with the then fashionable and newly wealthy writer Michael Arlen, who was persuaded to hand Noël a large cheque to ward off financial ruin and cover the cost of the production? And hadn't *The Vortex*'s dress rehearsal been the proverbial nightmare? Yet, Noël said, he had stuck to his conviction that it would be a hit and indeed it was. The same, he insisted, would happen with *Sirocco*. Again, Ivor said no.

So Noël said that if Ivor wouldn't do it he would play the part himself. Now, the idea of Noël Coward as a devilishly handsome and dashing young Italian waiter stretched credulity way beyond breaking point, and Ivor, in a misguided attempt to save his friend from total humiliation, agreed to star in it after all.

Noël was immensely relieved: after all he'd written the part with Ivor in mind, and expected the fact that he was Britain's leading silent-movie star to ensure a decent box office – whatever the critics might make of the play. Opposite Ivor, as

57

the young Englishwoman in love, was Frances Doble, then a very popular stage actress.

Unfortunately, once into rehearsal, the play lived down to all the worst fears that Novello had had when he first read it. He was, as he knew he would be, totally wrong for the part and this meant that he was himself part of the problem. Yes, he looked handsome; yes, he was a West End matinée idol with a huge fan club; and, yes, with his shock of jet-black hair he even looked like an Italian; but, as a red-blooded girl-bashing hetero Mediterranean, Ivor was simply unbelievable.

This was, let us remember, an actor whose stage reviews had included gems such as, 'he occasionally lost the heroic in the effeminate' and 'Mr Ivor Novello scarcely justified the villain's accusation of "vulgar manliness"'.

He was hopelessly miscast and the audience – or those in the cheaper seats, anyway – took against him from the start. There were catcalls when he appeared in what looked like silk pyjamas, and when he and Frances Doble had their first big love scenes the theatre was full of the sound of audience members making kissing noises.

At one point in the play Ivor threatens, 'I go to my mother!' Someone shouted out a helpful suggestion as to what he might do when he got there.

Those in the more expensive seats took issue with the ill manners of those in the cheaper – but they were of course sitting in the stalls and therefore vulnerable to dropped programmes and ice cream cartons as well as to insults from the galleries above.

Somehow the actors struggled through to the end of the play, but the curtain calls were mayhem, with an unprecedented level of booing drowning out the gallant cheers of Miss Doble's admirers in the stalls. So much for polite English audiences.

Never one to shirk a challenge when the theatre was concerned, Noël, waiting in the wings, saw and heard what was going on and, jaw clenched and eyes glittering with anger, he decided to go on and take the traditional author's curtain call, imagining that he could quiet the audience by sheer force of his personality.

He had plenty of opportunity to do so, as the director, Basil Dean, who had spent the whole performance at a nearby restaurant, glumly dining alone, sure of a disaster and wondering what his next directing work might be, had come back to Daly's Theatre in time for the curtain. Being rather deaf (a deaf director was only one of *Sirocco*'s many problems), he assumed that the jeers and boos were wild applause, so insisted that the stage manager keep raising the curtain for more calls, as if in triumph – an action that further infuriated the by now hysterical audience.

When Coward stepped onto the stage, in his solo act of defiance, all hell broke loose. Gallantly, he took Frances Doble's hand to lead her forward for another bow. Far from generating any admiration, he was met with the cry of 'Hide behind a woman, would yer?' Miss Doble had already had one direct contact with the audience during the night's performance, when someone, annoyed at the whistles her acting was producing from enemies in the circle, shouted out, 'Give the poor cow a chance!' 'Thank you, sir,' said Miss Doble, breaking out of character and walking to the front of the stage. 'You are the only gentleman here tonight!'

Now, as ice cream cartons rained down on her and the jeers increased in volume, she was in a state of hysterics, with tears pouring down her face. Mercifully resorting to autopilot as her spirits shrank from what was going on around her, she stuttered out, to the appalled fascination and then increased hilarity of the audience, her prepared curtain-call speech. 'Ladies and gentlemen,' she sobbed, helplessly. 'Tonight is the happiest night of my life!'

At this point Ivor – who, despite being very much a professional man of the theatre, always had a sense of humour and seemed to live by the maxims of Rudyard Kipling's poem 'If', treating both triumph and disaster as impostors not to be taken too seriously – burst out laughing. Noël refused to see the comedy in the situation, particularly as – on his way out of the stage door once the whole shambles had finally ended with the curtain staying firmly down and the actors mercifully allowed to leave the stage – he was spat on by a hostile crowd who had been waiting for him, and had to send his overcoat to the dry cleaners the next day.

He found sanctuary at the Ivy, where Ivor and the cast had already gone on ahead, and where they were indulging in some much-needed alcohol-fuelled letting down of hair. At this point even Noël relaxed and the nightmare was officially over.

As a result of that first night, *Sirocco* entered the West End language as a slang term for a disastrous opening performance – as in 'How did the show go last night!' '*Sirocco*, old boy, I'm afraid!' Ivor carried on in the role for the rest of its very short run but he and Noël Coward were never to work together again.

QUEEN MARY MEETS LILIAN BAYLIS

OLD VIC, 1930s

Two of the most formidable women of the twentieth century were bound to clash when they met – the irresistible force meeting the immovable object. Lilian Baylis, *Miss* Baylis to one and all, ran the Old Vic Theatre and, eventually, Sadler's Wells in Islington, an empire that she considered every bit as sacred a trust as running the nation.

One afternoon the redoubtable Queen Mary attended a gala matinée performance at the Old Vic and she was late. The Vic then specialised in first-class Shakespeare productions, which Miss Baylis had managed to achieve with a little money, a lot of artistic flair and, some thought, a hotline to the Almighty.

A devoted Anglican who attended Holy Communion on a more or less daily basis, she had a disconcerting habit of dropping to her knees in prayer, often in her office, where she was once heard to say to the Almighty, 'Dear God, please send me some good actors for this season – but make them cheap!'

Now, with no sign of the Queen's Daimler approaching, Miss Baylis was becoming agitated. She didn't believe in holding the curtain for anyone, however distinguished. She disapproved of her regulars (who were many, loyal and prompt) being kept waiting for the curtain to rise. Today, with a late royal party, she was forced to do so and she was very cross.

At last a couple of police motorbikes were spotted turning the corner towards the porticoed entrance of the Old Vic, and

61

the vast royal Daimler followed close behind, containing the Queen, her detective and a lady-in-waiting.

The Queen emerged from the car, wearing her trademark toque (a tall hat), which gave the illusion of height and added (as if it were needed) an even more regal touch. Toques had been in fashion over thirty years before, but, as King George V hated anything to do with the modern world (i.e. post-1910), the Queen was obliged to live, sartorially, in an Edwardian time warp.

Now the Queen was walking towards Miss Baylis. Miss Baylis dropped a suitably low curtsey, then broke all protocol by taking the Queen by the hand and saying, 'Come along, Your Majesty, we mustn't keep people waiting! I know it wasn't your fault, dear, the traffic has been terrible, but we should have started two minutes ago!'

(Queen Mary carried a handbag, of course – which was regularly checked by her ladies-in-waiting. Regal though she may have been, she suffered from a decided tendency towards kleptomania where *objets d'art* were concerned, and was the terror of West End antique dealers until they came to an informal arrangement whereby the ladies-in-waiting either surreptitiously returned the goods or arranged for them to be paid for.)

No one ever dared treat the Queen with anything less than total respect and according to the strictest protocol. However, none of the obsession with protocol was in evidence at the Old Vic that day. Rushing along to the royal box, Miss Baylis almost threw the Queen inside, adding – after she had nodded to the conductor in the orchestra pit, the signal for him to start the national anthem – 'Now we always play your husband's tune, dear, so I hope you'll feel at home!'

After the last bars of the anthem died away, the performance began, but for Queen Mary, at least, the most extraordinary part of the show had already taken place.

THE TRANSCONTINENTAL RAILROAD

CALIFORNIA, 1932

The train was picking up speed as it pulled out of Los Angeles. Its eventual destination: New York. On the train was the still youthful-looking (at 39) cinema star Ivor Novello. A year in Hollywood, this time as a writer rather than an actor, was all he could find. He had been a writer on the first talking Tarzan movie, *Tarzan of the Apes*, which just about summed up how ineptly the studio bosses were using his talent.

A sun lover all his life, he had enjoyed that side of California but, in his enforced and well-heeled leisure, waiting for someone, somehow, to actually use him, he had come up with a variety of ideas for new plays.

As the train passed through the Californian countryside, he was thinking of the cold and damp of the London to which he was now returning. But for him the weather was outweighed by the lure of the West End, his true spiritual – and commercial – world. He couldn't wait to get back, to return to the flat over the misleadingly named Strand Theatre (it wasn't in the Strand, it was in the nearby Aldwych).

One regret he had was not getting to know another English exile in California: Edgar Wallace, who had very recently come out to Hollywood. Wallace was a hugely popular crime novelist who churned out a staggering number of books. A *Punch* cartoon once showed a customer at a railway station newsstand asking, 'Have you got the midday Wallace?'

Wallace's novels were all very captivating – he was a racier, male version of Agatha Christie, thought Ivor – but what Ivor was really interested in was Wallace's theatre career. For Wallace had also (in a life that encompassed several different, and lucrative careers, all practised at the same time) been a very successful playwright and producer, working in partnership with Sir Gerald Du Maurier – these days mainly remembered as the father of novelist Daphne Du Maurier, but in the 1920s the leading man of the West End stage.

For a man like Ivor, who lived, breathed and dreamed theatre, having Edgar Wallace in town was a great relief, a little touch of London in the desert, a hint of stage doors and drizzly pavements among the cocktails and chatter of California.

The problem was, the men hardly overlapped. Ivor was already planning to leave when Wallace's arrival in Hollywood – he had the idea for the film *King Kong* – was announced. Nonetheless, hoping at least to catch a few minutes' chat with him, Ivor ensured that Wallace was invited to his farewell-to-Hollywood party.

Wallace, lonely without the company of his much younger second wife, back home in London with their daughter, would have been delighted to mingle with the stars, but felt very unwell, so sent a note to the Novello mansion to say he wasn't able to attend.

In fact he wasn't merely unwell: he was dying, of pneumonia, which he did on 10 February 1932. Ivor heard the news, was naturally sad, as well as disappointed that he never got to meet him, but soon put this out of his mind as he prepared to take the train to New York and then sail for home.

With him went his pet dog, and naturally enough the dog wasn't allowed to sit in the passenger compartment. So, having boarded, found his seat and settled, Ivor took the dog to the guard's luggage compartment, where the dog, with a bowl of water, plate of biscuits and several visits from Ivor, would remain for the duration of the journey.

As Ivor went to return to his seat the dog became upset and restless. 'Is it all right if I stay for while, just to settle him in?' Ivor asked the guard. 'Yes, sir, provided you don't mind the fact there ain't no chairs – or much room for that matter.'

'That's fine,' replied Ivor. 'I'll find somewhere to perch.' And, as the guard turned and left, he sat down on what looked and felt like a wooden container, covered by a simple, black blanket. Some time later the guard came back. 'Everything all right, sir?' 'Yes,' beamed Ivor. 'I'll go back to my seat soon. But I've been quite comfortable here. What is it?' he asked, seeing a look of surprise and discomfort on the guard's face. 'Erm . . . it's a coffin, sir.' 'Good heavens!' replied Ivor. 'What's it doing here? Whose is it?' 'It's going to London, sir,' replied the guard. 'And on the same liner as you, I believe. He was a theatrical gentleman, too. His name was Edgar Wallace.'

So, Ivor had Edgar's company after all – even if the conversation *was* a little one-sided.

A GLAMOROUS NIGHT – AND A TEA PARTY

DRURY LANE, 1935

King George V and Queen Mary arrived in the royal box at Drury Lane. The Queen felt a wave of relief at the fact that they had actually arrived. Her husband was not known for his interest in the theatre. Indeed, he had once been asked what his favourite play was. Lumping all performing arts together as 'a damned waste of time', he replied with an opera: '*La Bohème*. Easy choice. It's the shortest.'

It had been a miracle that the Queen had persuaded the King to go to the theatre, but this was his Silver Jubilee, the theatre was important, and the show was a new work, Ivor Novello's first musical, which combined beautiful women, fabulous tunes, lavish sets and, most importantly, a monarch and a royal court. Something that George would at least take an interest in. Though the Queen hoped he wouldn't spoil it by muttering about whether or not the uniforms were correct.

The royal couple stood at the front of the box for the national anthem, while the audience (it was a full house) stood to attention. After, as they sat down, the King looked noticeably more cheerful. A courtier had once asked him what his favourite tune was, and George replied, perfectly truthfully, 'God Save the King'.

The orchestra struck up the overture, a medley of gorgeous melodies that included the songs 'Fold Your Wings of Love Around Me' and 'Shine Through My Dreams', as well as a stirring military march. Ivor Novello's musical, in which, of course, he starred, was a wildly romantic tale that skilfully mingled Ruritanian fantasy with the modern world. That Novello was there, on stage, in a show he had devised and composed himself, was thanks to an extraordinary lunch at the Ivy – then, as now, London's premier theatre restaurant.

Ivor had been taken to lunch there by Harry Tennent, the theatre manager-producer who was also responsible for running Drury Lane. The Lane, he explained to Ivor, was in serious trouble. There hadn't been a major hit since *Cavalcade* in 1931, and now there was talk of its closing down.

'You *were* a composer, Ivor,' Harry said. 'There was "Keep the Home Fires Burning" and all those other songs during the war . . . What we need is a musical. A big musical. Couldn't you come up with something suitable?'

Ivor took the bait. If he could pull it off, this would be an amazingly lucky break. And a chance to top the success of *Cavalcade*'s writer – Noël Coward. Coward and Novello had long been friends, but were also (entirely unofficially, of course) major rivals. For Ivor to eclipse Noël, and at Drury Lane, would be too delicious for words. So he pretended that he did indeed have just such a musical in a drawer back home at the Aldwych.

Warming to his theme, he told Harry Tennent a story of a king and an opera singer who is his mistress, of a traitorous prime minister and a sinking cruise liner, a gypsy wedding and wicked assassins . . . By the time they reached dessert Ivor was bright-eyed with excitement and Tennent was hooked. 'Marvellous!' he said, 'Can you come round to meet the board of directors at the Lane in, say, two days' time? You can tell them all about it and play them the score. I'm sure they'll love it!'

Ivor gulped, smiled, and assured him that would be perfect. And then he spent the next 48 hours, kept awake and alert with gallons of black coffee, writing enough material to present to the directors. He managed to pull this off, the musical was accepted, and *Glamorous Night*'s first night lived up to its name – and was a huge success.

Hence the presence this evening of King George and Queen Mary. The Queen in particular was seen to watch intently as the action unfolded: Ivor playing a young television inventor (at a time when television had barely been heard of) who travels to a foreign country, Krasnia, where he arrives at the capital's opera house just in time to save a lovely opera singer, Militza (played by Mary Ellis), from being assassinated.

Despite her icy exterior, Queen Mary, like every other woman in the audience, couldn't help but identify with Miss Ellis as she was swept into Ivor's arms – not for nothing was he known as the most handsome man in England. She too was alarmed as the cruise liner the couple are travelling on is blown up by a bomb and sinks in full view of the audience, and felt relief when (without a hair out of place) they safely reach the nearest shore.

Once 'ashore', Ivor's and Ellis's characters are 'married' in a lavish gypsy ceremony but return to Krasnia to foil the prime minister's attempt to assassinate the King. Militza realises how much the King (whose mistress she had once been) needs her and decides she must marry him after all, keeping her gypsy wedding in that far-off land for ever a secret. The grateful King gives the inventor a cheque to fund his television station (this *has* to be the strangest plot of any musical!), on condition that the first outside broadcast be of his marriage to Militza. As in all the best dynasties (and this was, after all, the royals' Silver Jubilee year), duty is put before love.

As the curtain came down, the Queen was seen to wipe her eyes before joining the wave of applause that greeted the curtain call, as it had every night.

Some time later, Novello was invited to a garden party at Buckingham Palace – a sign of royal approval of his musical. He was presented to the King, who, rather than just nodding and uttering some bland comment about the weather, actually spoke to Ivor about his work – a very rare event between the King and anyone theatrical. 'A very good evening, Mr Novello,' the King said, 'but for your next musical, which I shall certainly come to, I want you to write a happier ending. You see, I don't like to see the Queen cry!'

Ivor wrote many more musicals, three of which opened at Drury Lane – *Careless Rapture* (1936), *Crest of the Wave* (1937) and *The Dancing Years* (1939) – but sadly King George was not to see any of them, as he died in January 1936.

THE NAZIS AT DRURY LANE

DRURY LANE, 1939

It's generally assumed that the Nazis never reached Britain during World War Two – well, apart from Rudolph Hess (who spent much of it in the Tower of London) and a few downed Luftwaffe pilots.

Yet, thanks to the playwright, actor and composer Ivor Novello, in a strange way they actually reached London before the war broke out, and toured the length and breadth of Britain during it.

This came about because Novello had been on holiday in Venice, where he arranged to meet up with a friend who was coming on from Vienna. The friend duly arrived, but looked distressed. 'What's the matter?' asked Ivor. 'Didn't you have a good time in Vienna? All that cake?'

'It's extraordinary,' the friend replied, 'But, now the Nazis have taken over the place, you can't buy records by Jewish composers.' Novello wasn't Jewish himself but the idea of a political regime persecuting artists – and an entire race – appalled him. It also gave him the germ of an idea for his new musical.

The following year, in March, *The Dancing Years* opened at Drury Lane. The main part of the show was a conventional love story between a young composer (Novello, aged 42, playing a twentysomething Rudi) and a beautiful opera singer Maria (played by Mary Ellis). Rudi and Maria fall in love, but split up over a mistakenly interpreted overheard remark and Maria rushes off to marry a Hapsburg prince (as one does). The trouble is, the child she eventually has, and whom Rudi meets years later, turns out to be Rudi's and not the prince's – a secret she and Rudi agree to keep. So far, so musical theatre. But the show all takes place in a flashback from a present-day scenario in which Ivor's character has been arrested by the Nazis for helping Jews escape from Austria to Switzerland. The show ends with him and Maria, who has engineered his release, talking about the dark days ahead and how music will keep the world sane.

The Drury Lane management and the government (especially the Foreign Office) begged Novello to remove the reference to the Nazis, but he refused – the only concession he made was to have the Nazis wear fairly neutral military uniforms so as not to upset the Third Reich too much.

As soon as war broke out the uniforms became unmistakably Nazi, and this element of the show – attacking Hitler's tyranny – helped make it enormously popular during the war. Drury Lane, like other London theatres, closed temporarily when war was announced, and, when it reopened soon after (as the government realised theatre's role in boosting morale), it was taken over by the armed services' entertainment organisation ENSA (Entertainments National Service Association, or 'Every Night Something Awful').

Novello is nowadays thought of primarily in terms of romance and escapism, but with *The Dancing Years* he wrote a surprisingly political piece of musical theatre and, though it remains largely forgotten today, it brought the Nazis – on stage – to England in the run-up to the real-life war that they precipitated.

A COMPOSER GOES TO PRISON

WORMWOOD SCRUBS, 1944

The large, black Humber police car drew up to the forbidding wooden gates of Wormwood Scrubs prison. The gates swung open, the car passed through, stopped before another set of iron gates and, once the wooden ones were safely closed behind it, the iron ones were open and the car moved forward.

Drawing up outside the reception office, a policeman emerged, and with him the prisoner: an immaculately groomed, middle-aged man. Although looking shocked and stricken at where fate had taken him, he retained the careless glamour and good looks that had smoothed his professional path in the cinema and theatre for the past 25 years.

His looks and his clothes were light years from the drab reality of the war that had been raging through Europe for five years and was to carry on for another twelve months or so. They were all the more out of place at a prison like Wormwood Scrubs.

He was taken in, met by the deputy governor and the chaplain – a fellow Welshman – and registered. He took a bath laced with disinfectant, changed into prison clothes – a suit far removed from his usual Savile Row clothing, and a shirt that would never have got through the doorway of the Jermyn Street shops he frequented.

Shown into his single cell (there was at least that consolation) he sat on the bed, the prison cocoa untasted in the mug on the scratched little bedside table. Staring at the bleak walls, he sat, staring straight ahead, seeing not the hideous present but the series of events that had led up to this, his own wartime drama.

The year was 1944 and the prison term given to this hugely popular star was for the terrible crime of – a petrol-coupon fraud. He was the only man ever to serve a prison sentence for this crime but everything about this event, including his trial and imprisonment, was bizarre.

He had been told, during the war, that he could no longer have the necessary petrol coupons for his Rolls-Royce (which drank gallons). The Rolls took him down to Redroofs, his Berkshire weekend country home. When he learned this would no longer be possible – that he would have to take the train like everyone else – he told his dressing room full of admirers that he may as well give it away.

One of them, a devoted female fan, said that she could have the car transferred to her firm, which was in Reading, and that the car would be put at his disposal when required – problem solved.

The star was delighted and agreed, though he insisted that his chauffeur should not lose his job, and to ensure the man's continued employment he would continue paying his salary.

It turned out that not only did the fan have no authority from the Reading firm to make the transfer but she was also fiddling the books and she got caught. As the result of someone else's shenanigans, the star composer was summoned to appear on a charge of conspiracy to flout the petrol-rationing regulations.

That was the problem – it wasn't that he'd flouted them but that he'd entered into a conspiracy to do so. A brilliant public performer, he was an atrocious court witness, panicked about dealing with real life (from which he'd been insulated by his talent and his wealth since his early twenties) and horrified at being out of the theatre and in court.

The fact that he tried to blame the woman for everything didn't go down well, either. The trial magistrate loathed the theatre and detested gays, and this gave him the opportunity to torment the man accused, who was an important member of both stage and homosexual communities, on both grounds. The female fan was fined just £50.

For the star it was different and devastating. The magistrate's eyes narrowed into vindictive slits as he pronounced sentence: 'The normal sentence for this offence would be a fine, but that would be little punishment for a man in your position. I hereby sentence you to two months in prison!'

He was given leave to appeal and did so. His friends tried to rally support: one of them, Sir Edward Marsh, who had been Winston Churchill's private secretary, even saw the prime minister, who expressed sympathy but could do nothing.

At the retrial it was decided to halve the sentence – to a month. He gave a theatrical gesture of despair to his friends in the courtroom and was then taken off to Wormwood Scrubs.

He was to come close to a nervous breakdown, but was saved by being put in charge of the prison choir, and consulted on the creation of a small theatre inside the prison – part of the attempted rehabilitation of prisoners. When he was released, it was at the stroke of midnight, to avoid the press, who were expected to gather at the gates at the normal release hour.

Emerging from the prison gates, back into the world, he was taken to a waiting car. As he shut the car door behind him, the theatrical atmosphere around this midnight flit amused him and a flash of his usual, camp humour returned: 'Good, heavens!' he said. 'It's like Marie Antoinette and the Flight to Varennes!'

As a result of his experiences in Wormwood Scrubs, he donated a piano to the prison, which can still be seen there in the chapel. He encouraged other stars to give concerts for the prisoners, although he never performed there himself and never visited. While he continued to perform and write musicals for Drury Lane, he never fully recovered from the experience and died relatively young, aged 58.

His name was Ivor Novello.

DOLORES GRAY AT THE COLISEUM

LONDON COLISEUM, 1947

There have been many memorable first nights at the London Coliseum, Oswald Stoll's flagship theatre, which opened in 1904. Built by arguably Britain's greatest ever theatre architect, Frank Matcham, the Coliseum was designed as a variety theatre, and staged a vast number of shows there (often twice a day) as well as ballet, including Diaghilev's legendary Ballets Russes.

It has also been a cinema and, since the late 1960s, the home of English National Opera and English National Ballet, formerly London's Festival Ballet. However, it has also been a major venue for musicals (and indeed ENO put on a highly praised production of Bernstein's *On the Town* in 2005, choreographed by Stephen Mears). In 1947, one of its most popular opened at the Coli, offering a postwar breath of fresh air straight across the Atlantic from the wide-open spaces of the American West.

Irving Berlin's *Annie Get Your Gun* had opened on Broadway on 16 May 1946, the title role of Annie Oakley, the Wild West sharpshooter, written for Ethel Merman. Merman wasn't interested in taking the show to London, however, so the hunt was on for a replacement.

The girl who won the role was much younger and better-looking than Merman. Her name was Dolores Gray, and she was statuesque. That isn't a polite word for fat: she was tall and athletic and most of her obituaries, when she eventually died in 2002, referred to her as 'Junoesque', suggesting she was like a female Roman statue. And she had a voice that was softer, richer, more melodic than Merman's – but just as loud.

Getting the part hadn't been easy. Oscar Hammerstein, co-writer and co-producer with his partner Richard Rodgers, hadn't at first taken to Dolores, but Mary Martin (a Rodgers and Hammerstein favourite) insisted that Dolores be given another try. Dolores was later to recall what happened:

> I sang twelve bars of 'How Deep is the Ocean' when he interrupted and said, 'That's enough!' He gave me a script to read and told me to come back the next day. I did so, with no make-up, hair pulled back, plainly dressed and carrying a broom handle as if it were a gun . . . I read and sang for them in the theatre for an hour, after which I was exhausted.

Josh Logan, the play's director, came down the aisle to the front of the stage to congratulate her and Hammerstein went into the theatre office, taking Dolores by the hand with him. There he sent a cable to the London producers, saying, 'We Have Just Found Annie'.

Annie Get You Gun opened at the Coliseum on 7 June 1947, which was Dolores Gray's 23rd birthday. The audience loved the show, giving it a standing ovation that seemed to go on for ever. In the course of a curtain speech (a theatrical tradition that has now sadly disappeared), the audience were told that it was Dolores Gray's birthday, and they immediately burst into a rendition of 'Happy Birthday', which had her standing there, at the front of the stage, facing that vast auditorium full of people standing in her honour, singing to her, as the tears flowed down her cheeks. It was not only the Coliseum's most extraordinary first night, but was Miss Gray's most memorable birthday, and the start of a love affair between her and the West End that was to have its last fling forty years later, when she appeared in the London production of Stephen Sondheim's *Follies*, singing that showbiz anthem 'I'm Still Here'. If only she were.

(See also 'Opening the Coliseum: Two Technical Disasters'.)

76

LIKE FATHER, LIKE SON . . .

FORTUNE THEATRE, 1947

Suppose you are a good-looking, heterosexual, 21-year-old male and the year is 1935; what is your dream job? Many, if not most, young men of the time wouldn't have had to think twice: a stagehand at the Windmill Theatre, Soho. The Windmill specialised in nude tableaux, naked young women who, when the curtain went up, were discovered in various poses but didn't move. Stationary, they classified as 'art', just like classical sculpture, whereas moving nudes were, of course, considered to be pornography. The men who came to see them in hordes didn't care whether they moved or not. The Windmill 'girls' proved enormously popular and during World War Two the Windmill boasted 'We Never Close' – and, despite the threat of bombs, the audience packed the theatre's five shows a day, their lust consistently triumphing over the Luftwaffe.

One of the lucky men who held that job, courtesy of a family friend, went on to be one of our best-loved actors. He had been born into a middle-class family in 1914, and had been unable to settle into a steady job until he found his vocation as a stage hand at the Windmill Theatre, a dream job only rudely interrupted by the advent of war.

He spent his war years in the Royal Navy, an excellent training for many of the gentlemanly stage and screen roles he was later to play. After the war, he started his career in theatre and was to appear in it throughout his working life, despite a major film career. In 1946 he appeared in *And No Birds Sing* at the Aldwych – playing a young clergyman. The following year he was in *Power Without Glory* at the Fortune. Another young actor in the production was Dirk Bogarde. Both men were admired, and pursued, by Noël Coward, who was then appearing in his own play, *Present Laughter*, at the Theatre Royal, Haymarket. Had the movies not intervened, he would still have made a fine career on stage playing decent, stiff-upper-lipped but basically humorous and kindly characters, until the onset of the Parkinson's disease that killed him in 1982 made stage appearances impossible.

Kenneth More is today remembered as a film star from the 1950s, largely thanks to roles in *Genevieve* (1953), *Doctor in the House* (1954), *Reach For the Sky* (1956) and an early and very good film about the *Titanic* disaster, *A Night to Remember* (1958).

It is doubtful whether Coward actually succeeded in capturing Dirk Bogarde in his amorous net, though he was later to joke about the latter's availability. In 1955, seeing a poster for *The Sea Shall Not Have Them*, starring Michael Redgrave and Dirk Bogarde, he quipped, 'I fail to see why not. Everyone else has!'

Kenny More was a different matter, though, and we know exactly what happened to Coward's seduction plan, because both of them talked about it until they died. Noël sent a note round to the Fortune stage door, with an invitation to dinner at his Belgravia home. More duly though nervously accepted, worried (quite rightly) that rather more than dinner might be on the agenda. Sure enough, Coward, after the two men had had a highly enjoyable meal littered with theatrical anecdotes and shared notes about life at sea, made a pass at the very heterosexual More.

What was he to do? Here was one of the most famous, and most influential, men in the theatre, at the head of the profession in which More was an ambitious young actor. He knew exactly how much help Coward could give him, were he disposed to do so, and exactly how much damage he could do if offended. Yet he simply couldn't go along with what Coward clearly wanted. How was he to get out of this potentially very tricky situation?

Eventually he hit on a solution. 'Oh, Mr Coward,' he said, 'I couldn't . . . I couldn't possibly have an affair with you! You see, sir, you remind me of my father!' Coward's eyes flickered, as he wrestled between disappointment and amusement.

More waited for a second that seemed an age. After a brief struggle Coward's good humour won through – quite possibly because, although he couldn't resist the temptation, he found passion, especially with essentially straight men, to be more of a burden than a pleasure. Finally, the Master spoke: 'Hello, Son!' he responded, and they greeted one another with 'Hello, Son!' whenever they met ever after. The phrase became an in-joke between them over the many years of their friendship. More's honour was saved, and the evening ended amicably though platonically.

VIVIEN LEIGH IN A STREETCAR NAMED DESIRE

ALDWYCH THEATRE, 1949

The scene: the Aldwych Theatre, one of London's most attractive Victorian playhouses. It had been home in the 1920s to playwright Ben Travers's Aldwych Farces and therefore a centre of London's light-comedy scene.

The date: 12 October 1949. The last month of autumn and the herald of winter in a period – postwar austerity – that was proving harsher, in terms of rationing and daily life, than it had been even during the war (other than the time of the Luftwaffe's bombs and doodlebugs, of course).

The event: the first night of Tennessee Williams's steamy Southern drama, *A Streetcar Named Desire*.

The actress: Vivien Leigh.

The role: that of Blanche Du Bois, of which Vivien Leigh, Lady Olivier, was later to say 'it was playing Blanche that drove me into madness'.

Blanche, a sexually voracious spinster past her prime but with enough vestiges of youthful beauty for her to pretend that she still has it, comes to a seedy tenement in New Orleans, to visit her sister, Stella, now living with her working-class husband, Stanley Kowalski.

The sisters were originally from a grand Southern plantation-house-owning family, but the money is long since gone – to the disbelief and fury of Stanley. Added to these feelings are his dislike of Blanche's airs and graces, a dislike that is blended with lust that explodes into rape. Blanche, deranged by this, is

80

taken off to a mental home while her sister refuses to believe her rape claim, because to do so would mean her having to leave Stanley, to whom she is in sexual thrall. She watches pitifully but helplessly as her sister is escorted away. As she leaves, Blanche utters one of Tennessee Williams's best-known lines: 'I have always depended on the kindness of strangers.'

To modern-day audiences, aware of Leigh's private life from the many accounts over the years, this is a first night with tragic implications, because the role in so many ways mirrored her own life – at least there was enough similarity to be striking, and to tip her into what she called madness. Vivien, like Blanche, came from a wealthy family, and she too grew up in heat and splendour, but hers was of the British Raj, not America's Deep South.

She was sent to a convent school outside London, from which her doting father eventually rescued her, in effect educating her himself with a series of grand tours of the Continent, during which she learned not just a facility for languages but a very refined appreciation of music and art.

Her first marriage was to a barrister called Leigh Holman, who, when she met him, was already going out with another girl. Vivien, however, didn't let anything like another young woman's feelings stand in her way. This marriage produced a daughter, Suzanne, but ended in divorce.

The great love of her life, though, was Laurence Olivier, with whom she had an affair, then lived, and finally married in 1940. The two were to become the golden couple of the British stage, acting together in numerous plays (they took *Hamlet* to Elsinore in 1937, Vivien playing Ophelia to Larry's Hamlet).

Their twenty-year run as the Oliviers came to an end in 1960 with their divorce. He subsequently married Joan Plowright; she lived with the actor Jack Merivale in an apartment in Eaton Square, where she died, tragically early, in 1967, aged 53.

All this may seem a far cry from a distressed spinster down on her luck, her money and her looks, but for Vivien, as she took her curtain call that autumn evening at the Aldwych, the similarities were all too close – and were to get much more so as the run (and then the film, with Marlon Brando) continued. And for us, with the benefit of hindsight, they are even clearer.

Vivien was a great beauty in her youth, but over the years her looks turned quite matronly, even though her eyes kept their fierce sparkle and her skin its amazing complexion. But time was no more kind to her than to any other great beauty, and, eleven years after she had triumphed as Ophelia in the very castle where *Hamlet* was set, she was considered too old to play the part in Larry's film version in 1948.

Her manic depression, which took the form of extreme overexcitability and a voracious sexual appetite saw her, on occasion, disappear to wander the streets and public parks in search of casual sex – a very graphic version of needing 'the kindness of strangers'.

This resulted in many episodes of hospitalisation over the years, and also saw her receive regular doses of ECT – electroconvulsive therapy.

Blanche Du Bois's mental problems are exacerbated by her losing her looks, her position in life and her status. Vivien, though never poor, felt the loss of her marriage to Laurence Olivier very keenly, and always kept a picture of him in her bedroom. Indeed, when she died, Jack Merivale, phoning Sir Laurence to break the news, still referred to her as 'Lady Olivier'.

Tennessee Williams brilliantly caught the delicate but distressed state that enabled Blanche to carry on functioning – and to attract men – but that was so fragile that almost anything, let alone a rape, could shatter it. He did, however, in an equally telling scene, give her a certain inner strength and the ability to reach into herself and find some sort of dignity, however harrowing her circumstances – hence her pulling herself together when she is about to be led off to the mental hospital.

The doctor in charge of her is a kind man – in contrast with the rather brutal nurse who accompanies him – and realises that the best way to pacify Blanche and get her to go quietly, is to treat her as a lady, So, rather than restrain her, he offers her his arm, and she then comes out with the famous line about strangers.

Vivien Leigh depended on the kindness of friends, and,

though her manic episodes often exasperated them, John Gielgud and Noël Coward in particular offered her friendship, comfort and a place to stay when things got too much for her – as they often did, even at her own equivalent of Blanche's family mansion, the Oliviers' country house, Notley Abbey. All too often Olivier, exhausted from a week that had seen eight shows a week in a gruelling Shakespearean production, would just want to go to bed after dinner and get some sleep, Vivien would be determined to keep him and the house guests up half the night playing games, chatting or drinking.

These episodes, which became more frequent as she grew older and the marriage became more strained, were often and unsurprisingly made worse by the frequent sniping at her stage performances by the critic Kenneth Tynan. Tynan, very much a ladies' man, nonetheless had an almost sexual admiration for and interest in Laurence Olivier, and was to work with him as literary manager at the National Theatre in the decade before it finally moved into its current home on the South Bank.

During the 1950s, however, he was the country's most fashionable and feared theatre critic, and Vivien's peace of mind was not exactly helped by Tynan's habit of praising Olivier while slamming Leigh.

It was largely thanks to these consistently hostile reviews that the legend grew up of Olivier as a genius, held back and damaged by having to appear in stage productions with a wife whose talent was nowhere near his own, and whom he happily left behind at home when he made his films.

The truth was very different, and Vivien Leigh was a great stage actress – albeit in a rather old-fashioned way that might not find favour today – but she was also, undoubtedly, a star, and one of the reasons audiences went to see the Oliviers in the theatre. Her ability on stage was proved by the first night of *Streetcar*, which was a personal triumph for her, and led to the iconic film version a couple of years later, in 1951 – and for which she won her second Oscar as Best Actress. Little did she and the audience who rose to their feet in appreciation of her performance realise exactly how far her stage role would be mirrored in her real life.

THE LAST TRAIN TO BRIGHTON

LONDON TO BRIGHTON, 1950s

The comedian Max Miller had been born in Brighton in the mid-1890s and he was still living there in the 1950s, as were many other well-known performers from Laurence Olivier to Dora Bryan. Brighton, then as now, had elegant Georgian houses, good antique shops in The Lanes, and the beautiful Theatre Royal. Hardly surprising, then, that it was the address of choice for a number of successful former Londoners. They all took the fast late-night train from Victoria after their shows and congregated in the bar, where they told each other how their performances had gone that evening, who had been in the audience, what the gossip was on Shaftesbury Avenue and who was likely to get which role in which play.

As they neared Brighton the talk got livelier and louder, thanks to the post-performance champagne favoured by most of them, and they vied with one another to tell the best or most scandalous anecdote. The stars were relaxed, among their own kind, and at their best.

Sharing the bar and listening quietly was a distinguished gentleman in a very good suit whom none of the others knew. Over the years, being English, the actors unbent enough to give a civil nod in the gent's direction before they started drinking, and even proffered the occasional 'Good evening. Have a pleasant day?' to which the quiet gent replied with a self-effacing murmur before ordering his usual stiff whisky and sitting silently listening to the theatrical chatter.

One evening, as soon as they were all gathered in the bar, the quiet man held up his hand, indicating that he wanted their attention. The actors were shocked into silence. He had purchased a number of bottles of the railway's very best champagne and, while they watched him, intrigued, he poured a glass for each of them.

'Now,' he said, 'I'd like you all to have a drink with me because I retired today. For forty years I've worked for a firm that makes ball bearings, the last fifteen as the managing director. Today was my last day.' Feeling pretty trapped, the actors, having accepted the man's champagne, nevertheless collectively decided, without discussing it, that politeness demanded they ask him something about his life in ball bearings.

For the next hour and a quarter, the entire length of the journey from Victoria to Brighton, the quiet man, who had never before spoken, told Laurence Olivier, Max Miller, Dora Bryan and all the others about ball bearings – how they are made, how they are marketed, how they are advertised, how many are sold and to whom, what they are used for, who uses them. He didn't vary his topic. By the time they pulled into the station, every one of them was glazed beyond boredom and had the journey been longer might have committed, if not murder, then suicide.

As the train stopped, the quiet man put on his hat, then raised it to his exhausted audience: 'Pretty boring, huh?' he goaded them. 'Well, then, can you imagine the excruciating, unadulterated, murderous tedium *I* have endured every single night for the past fifteen years listening to *you*?'

With that, he replaced his hat and vanished into the Brighton night.

SIR CHARLES B COCHRAN GETS INTO HOT WATER

HYDE PARK HOTEL, 1951

Which theatrical celebrity had the most bizarre or painful death? There are several candidates – actors who were murdered, Isadora Duncan, whose long scarf caught in the wheels of her car while she was driving, James Dean's debatable suicide, Orson Welles's death from overindulgence – but Sir Charles Cochran would be my choice.

He was one of early-twentieth-century Britain's leading impresarios, famous for his revues, and their endless string of bright, blonde 'Cochran's Young Ladies', many of whom he enjoyed personally as well as professionally.

Described as 'An English Diaghilev', he had a talent for spotting new artists and mixing them with other creatives to produce lively, good-looking shows that appealed to the public taste.

His collaboration with the young Noël Coward was to result in *Bitter Sweet*, *Cavalcade* and *Private Lives*, while he also presented Russian ballet dancers, rodeos, boxing and stage giants like Sarah Bernhardt and Eleonora Duse.

Among those whose careers he either made or boosted were Gertrude Lawrence, Evelyn Laye, Jessie Matthews (who stole Laye's husband), Beatrice Lillie and the fragrant Anna Neagle. Among the designers he used (echoes of Diaghilev and Bakst) were Cecil Beaton, Oliver Messel and Augustus John. Frederick Ashton and William Walton worked on Cochran productions and 'Cockie', as he was affectionately known, also presented Cole Porter's *Nymph Errant* in London.

He was a stickler for stage discipline, and expected Cochran's Young Ladies to look and act like ladies off stage as well as in the theatre. He could be very generous – when one of his chorus girls fainted during a rehearsal he sent the entire cast into a local restaurant with orders to make sure they all ate a steak – but had an infuriating habit of changing the running orders of the revues, often on a whim. On one memorable occasion the leading man, who should have appeared on stage dressed like Fred Astaire in white tie and tails, actually had to go on and dance, thanks to a last-second change in the running order, in a full suit of armour.

Cochran's was a remarkable life, with its bankruptcies as well as its luxury hotels and the inevitable rivers of champagne. But what is most extraordinary, in an admittedly rather macabre way, is how Cochran died. It was a tragedy, in that it was avoidable, and involved a fair amount of bad luck, and it reads today like the sort of health-and-safety warning that seems to appear everywhere (like little notices on bags of peanuts, saying, 'Beware! May contain nuts'!).

Cochran, in January 1951, was aged 78 but still producing often, with ideas for new projects all the time. He was faced with the more practical problem, recently, of repairs to his and his wife's flat in Chesham Street, so Sir Charles and Lady (Evelyn) Cochran moved into the Hyde Park Hotel, a large and very grand hotel in Knightsbridge, much favoured by the grander literary and theatrical set – Evelyn Waugh was a regular there.

Sir Charles suffered terribly from osteoarthritis, and found that he gained some measure of relaxation from a warm bath. This was usually run for him, and carefully checked for temperature, by his wife. On 22 January, early in the morning, he decided to run it himself, because they had both had a bad night's sleep and he thought she could do with the rest. This act of husbandly gallantry was to be the death of him.

He went into the bathroom, and filled the bath half full of water before getting into it. Perhaps because he thought the maid might come into the bedroom, he had decided to lock the bathroom door. This too, was an act of chivalry – sparing the maid's blushes – that was to play a vital part in the disaster.

After lowering himself into the bath as well as he could, given the arthritis, he turned off the cold tap, since the water wasn't quite warm enough. He left the hot tap running. Comfortably settled in the vast bath, he then found that the water *was* warm enough; in fact, the hot-water tap was piping hot and had very quickly raised the temperature. He went to turn it off but, to his horror, the arthritis had locked his hip in place. He couldn't move. Meanwhile the water got hotter and hotter . . .

He might have alerted his wife with his screams straightaway, had the maid not (further tragedy) chosen to start the vacuum cleaner outside their bedroom door just at that moment. Eventually Lady Cochran woke up, as the scream of agony broke through her sleep and drowned out even the noise of the hoover.

Assuming the noise was coming from the street, she got out of bed, walked to the window and looked out, but after a couple of minutes the noise was getting worse, not better, yet there was no sign of any commotion in the street at all.

Suddenly, she realised, to her horror, that the noise was coming from the bathroom. She went to open the door but found it was locked. Cochran managed to scream out to her what had happened, and she summoned help. Eventually the hotel porter, plus a couple of nearby guests who had also heard the noise, managed to break the impressively heavy and secure door open. The tap was turned off and Cochran's appallingly scalded body – all modesty now long forgotten – was gingerly removed from the almost boiling water, amid clouds of dense steam.

Although he lingered for over a week, he died in Westminster Hospital, on 31 January 1951. The one good thing to come out of this appalling tragedy was that Lady Cochran had been able to offer him some much-needed comfort on her last visit to him, not long before the end. He was lying in bed, terribly burned, and dozy with the vast amounts of morphine needed to keep him comfortable.

'Cockie,' she asked him, 'do you know what happened to you?'

'No,' he muttered, as the trauma had been wiped from his memory, largely thanks to the morphine.

'You must close your eyes,' she continued. 'You've had an operation [for the arthritis] and you're cured. Close your eyes and when you wake you'll never feel any pain again.'

When he died, a memorial plaque was placed in the actors' church, St Paul's, Covent Garden. Like many of the other plaques there it has a quotation from Shakespeare on it and, as with the others, it was well chosen: what better epitaph for the man whose talent brought together so many great actors and singers, and who heard so many cheers of approval at so many opening nights, than these from *Coriolanus*? 'I thank you for your voices, thank you, your most sweet voices.'

GIELGUD'S RHODESIAN RICHARD II

BULAWAYO, ZIMBABWE, 1953

The year was 1953, the year in which Elizabeth II was crowned at Westminster Abbey, the television age (in Britain at any rate) began, and perhaps the greatest British actor of all-time was made a knight of the realm by the new Queen.

Unfortunately, this was also to be the year of his arrest for importuning in a public lavatory, a crime of which he was found guilty and fined. The arrest, the court case and the resulting publicity were an enormous embarrassment, of course, but he rose above it, thanks to his usual whirlwind of work.

That work encompassed both film and stage, though it was for the stage that he was best-known (film fame came relatively late, in his sixties), and Shakespearean stage at that.

His two most famous roles to date had been those of Hamlet, which he played many times in several productions, and Richard II, the aesthete king. Both parts suited his exquisite stage presence, his sense of poetry and that marvellous, silvery voice. But as he grew older he decided to retire them both. Richard had been a role that suited him well, and that his public expect him to reprise, but, as with Hamlet, he eventually felt that he was flogging, if not a dead horse, then a decidedly tired one that would be better suited to grazing in retirement pastures.

But, after his arrest and the subsequent desire to get away from the flurry of interest in his private life, he decided to accept the invitation of the then colonial government of

Rhodesia (renamed Zimbabwe after official independence in 1980), to celebrate the Rhodes Centenary Festival – Cecil Rhodes having founded the country and given it his name. What they wanted was his production of *Richard II*, a role he had said he had no intention of ever playing again.

It was to be his last and best performance as Richard, a part he made famous not just in Shakespeare's play but in Gordon Daviot's very popular *Richard of Bordeaux*, and it took place not in some glamorous West End playhouse but in a small theatre in the depth of the Rhodesian countryside – in Bulawayo.

He was, of course, Sir John Gielgud, and, in these supremely gentle, poetic roles such as Richard, he was incomparable. Not all his friends thought the decision a wise one – he was, after all, pushing fifty and playing a twentysomething king. However, he justified the decision with the rather pessimistic thought, 'When one reckons that one has only, at the most, six or seven more highly active years in the theatre, one must organise life to do as many things as one feels like.'

The theatre in Bulawayo was made of corrugated iron, without any of the amenities that Gielgud took for granted in the West End and on Broadway. But, in the worst of all possible worlds, Gielgud (who was directing the production as well as playing Richard) found that the primitive playhouse boasted a stage that was 'as wide as the Festival Hall in London . . . it still takes us five minutes, or so it seems, to cross [it]'.

Playing the gorgeously attired king, the epitome of medieval monarchy, in these bizarre circumstances did nothing for his self-confidence and gave a fresh melancholy to the words 'For God's sake let us sit upon the ground, and tell sad stories of the death of kings' (Act III, Scene II). His king didn't die – audiences, starved of great, or indeed any, Shakespeare, lapped it up – but on this occasion he felt a terrible sense of being at odds with the play, the character and the time.

When he had first played Richard in 1929 he had closely identified not only with the role but also with the man:

I seemed to be immediately in sympathy with that strange mixture of weakness and beauty in the character . . . As soon as I began to study the part myself, the subtlety of Shakespeare's characterisation began to fascinate and excite me . . . Richard was such a shallow, spoiled young man, vain of his looks, with lovely things to say. I found myself no end in the part, but even that seemed to help my acting of it . . . I began to feel that I had made a real personal success . . .

Now, in 1953, he thought he was, after all, too old to play the role – 'I could only imitate the performance I gave as a young man' – but he played the part with as much of the old magic as he could, even if it was now a flickering flame rather than the earlier searchlight that had illuminated one of Shakespeare's greatest roles and brought to life the medieval world that the play recreated in all its glory – and danger.

Richard II in Bulawayo was performed to a mainly white audience, though blacks were allowed into a separate area of the auditorium. This may have been colonial Africa but it wasn't the apartheid of neighbouring South Africa. Nonetheless, Gielgud – the most nonpolitical and theatre-fixated actor alive (he had greeted news of the fall of France with the shocked announcement that Gladys Cooper seemed to have had terrible reviews for her latest play) – realised that this was inappropriate in the postwar world, and asked to meet some of the black members of the audience after the curtain call.

This was duly arranged, with some of the prettiest black girls in the audience being lined up to meet him in his dressing room. Either the authorities thought he had an eye for the ladies or, more likely, knew he had one for the lads and were determined to keep him from corrupting any nice young black men who had come to the show.

In any case, this demonstration of racial – if not class – solidarity was somewhat dented when the girls who were duly presented to him dropped him a low curtsey. It's been argued that this defeated the racial gesture, in that he was being treated like any other very important white man in Rhodesia.

I prefer to think, however, that, despite the various drawbacks of this not so much provincial as positively bush theatre, and the insecurities prompted by his being too old for the part, Gielgud's extraordinary stage presence triumphed after all. I hope that his particular affinity for this role and the effort he put into redefining it for a new public (at London rehearsals the cast had regularly been brought to tears by his performance) had so moved his audience that, even with the lights up, the curtain down and the makeup removed, when they came face to face with him they saw not a middle-aged actor but, as Shakespeare had made him, the embodiment of kingship. In which case, knighthood or no, a curtsey was entirely appropriate, and a tribute to art rather than empire.

CAMERON MACKINTOSH AND SALAD DAYS

VAUDEVILLE THEATRE, 1954

A little boy was taken by a favourite aunt to see a West End show to celebrate his eighth birthday. Son of a Scottish father and a Maltese mother, he was dressed in his best kilt with all the trimmings, a little lace shirt and a miniature sporran. He looked very smart but he wasn't all that impressed with going to a musical, which seemed to him rather a girly thing to do. But he loved his auntie and she wanted to see the latest hit, which had opened to rave reviews on 5 August 1954, so he gallantly pretended that he wanted to be in the Vaudeville Theatre that afternoon.

The show was *Salad Days*, Julian Slade's quintessentially English musical about youth and innocence, about hope for the future and belief in oneself, about looking forward and, with the help of a little magic, dancing into a better world. The magic came from an onstage piano whose music made everybody want to dance. It appeared to play itself, although the music was actually coming from a pianist playing in the pit.

The little boy was entranced, fascinated by the piano and desperate to know how it worked. As soon as the curtain calls were over, he ran down the aisle to see if he could work out how a piano could play itself. Fortunately for him (and for us), the composer, Julian Slade, was himself playing the matinée that day and he was touched by the insistence of the small child to try to understand his world. He showed him not only the

94

mechanical piano but also how the curtain went up and how the lights went on and off by remote control.

Every oak tree, however magnificent, starts from an acorn, and every producer, however impressive, and however global his reach, starts as a boy. This boy needed only this backstage tour of the Vaudeville Theatre to turn him into a producer. This boy decided there and then that he wanted to stage musicals; he understood, before he ever knew the word, what a producer does and that he wanted to be one. Not be *in* the shows, as the romantic lead, but to *produce* them.

While he was still at his boys' school, he produced several shows – he still has the programmes – with his school friends as cast, crew, technicians, programme sellers and ticket takers (he was always professional). Once through with school, he tried drama school but found it too slow. He needed to learn his trade, which he did the hard way, working as a stage hand at Drury Lane, and then producing a number of disasters and semi-disasters before he learned to hedge his bets. The young producer made a lot of bad decisions as all young producers do, but all the shows he produced he loved and believed in, a continuing commitment to this day.

One that went belly-up early was a production of Cole Porter's *Anything Goes*, so it was all the more pleasing for him, years later, when, in 2004, he transferred Trevor Nunn's National Theatre production of the same show to the Theatre Royal Drury Lane, where it had a hugely successful run.

He got better at his job, never being deflected, never producing work he didn't like, occasionally having a minor hit. And then, in 1979, a young composer called Andrew Lloyd Webber, who had had two big hits with Tim Rice but who had been turned down by all the producers in London and New York because his current idea seemed so loony, knocked on his door. Andrew wanted to make a musical from T S Eliot's *Old Possum's Book of Practical Cats*, using the original poems as his lyrics.

Cats opened at the New London Theatre in May 1981, and was to run there for 21 years, entering the theatrical stratosphere and breaking all the records. We took our children and our grandchildren; we went and visited it from time to time like visiting a cherished old family friend. The producer became a millionaire, as did all his loyal creative staff who had taken a little piece of the show when the money ran out.

Other triumphs followed (and a few, a very few, disasters), among them *The Phantom of the Opera, Les Misérables, Side By Side By Sondheim, The Card, Martin Guerre, Five Guys Named Moe, Miss Saigon* and a project very dear to his heart, a revival of the first show he ever worked on at the Theatre Royal, Drury Lane, when he was a stagehand: Lionel Bart's *Oliver!*, then starring Ron Moody. It is an astonishing achievement, as is his most recent hit, a co-production with Disney of a stage musical version of *Mary Poppins*. And it all began back in 1954, with a wide-eyed boy being taken to see *Salad Days*.

His name is, of course, Sir Cameron Mackintosh, Britain's (if not the world's) most spectacularly successful producer, commercially and artistically. The theatre world on both sides of the Atlantic would have been unimaginably different if, for his eighth birthday, his auntie had decided on a toy car or a trip to the funfair. It is given to few of us to change our chosen world for ever and we are fortunate that, in Cameron Mackintosh, he changed it for the better and put the English musical on the map. This is what he set out to do, and at least the theatre, as Cameron Mackintosh has shown in spectacular style, can sometimes make dreams come true, with or without a magic piano.

KENNETH WILLIAMS IN ST JOAN

ARTS THEATRE, LONDON, 1954

There are times when the best thing that can happen to an actor is also the worst. Kenneth Williams was a deeply troubled man who believed that he would never be allowed by his reputation and audience to veer from the camp, outrageous, gay persona that he himself cultivated.

He saw himself as a serious actor, one who could play the delicate comedic timing that made his appearances on Tony Hancock's radio and television series and the endless lavatory jokes of the *Carry On* films so funny, but one who could just as well play a serious role in a classic play. He believed, rightly as it turned out, that the profession with whom he always had a love–hate relationship would not allow him to go back and forth.

Williams had an instantly recognisable voice – entirely constructed and false – that many of us remember from our childhood. It was nasal, mock-posh, with timing all its own. Like Peter Cook's E L Wisty voice, it was entirely unique and we knew from the first syllable who it was and that it, alone, independent of what it said, would make us laugh.

Thanks to the many reissues of the *Carry On* films, in which he was a major participant, and the CDs of his radio work, he seems never to have left us, and many younger people who were born after his death in 1988 are fervent fans.

His father, Charlie, was a barber in Marchmont Street, not far from Euston Station. Charlie never took to his only son and made no secret of his preference for his daughter, Pat. Kenneth was a small, thin, delicate and effeminate child, who from an early age 'put on' the clipped accent of the upper classes – or, rather, something that approximated to it and that, like his general demeanour, was something of a caricature.

Williams was later to get his own back on his unsympathetic father, a belated revenge for all those tirades that he painfully quotes in his autobiography: 'Get a trade, boy! Acting isn't reliable and in any case the women are all sluts and the men are all pansies!' It was a wickedly accurate parody in a comedy sketch with Peter Cook in which he played a demented barber. Charlie's hairdressing salon eventually went bust, which, from Kenneth's description of his father's attitude to his customers, is hardly surprising. Apparently, he often turned down customers' requests for hairdos that he thought inappropriate, 'Henna rinse? On you? You'd look like a tart!' With Kenneth's caustic and often wounding sense of humour and his unfortunate habit of alienating his best friends, it sounds as if the apple didn't fall far from the tree.

Williams's relationship with his mother, Louisa, was much closer. He ate with her most days and took her on holiday, cruises being a favourite way of seeing the world without too close a contact with foreign food or foreigners.

But even Charlie was impressed when, in the early 1950s, Kenneth began to get very small parts in films (The *Carry On* ones didn't start until 1959). Kenneth, however, saw film as a stepping stone towards a major part in a play, preferably a George Bernard Shaw play in a West End theatre. That, he thought, would be a real achievement.

Shaw was the first playwright whose work the young Kenneth had seen and he remained his favourite, as he was to recall in his autobiography:

We saw Shaw's *The Doctor's Dilemma*. I was entranced and fascinated. Never before had I heard such lively argument and such irreverent wit. I was shocked and attracted by the figure of Dubedat – his contemptuous dismissal of materialism and his impassioned plea for art found an immediate response in me. This was the sort of part I wanted to play – these were the aesthetics I wanted to proclaim.

After this theatrical revelation, he read all of Shaw's plays, and the friend who'd taken him to see *The Doctor's Dilemma* (they both worked at Stanford's, the map makers in Long Acre) also gave him a copy of Shaw's *Prefaces*. Kenneth had, he hoped, found his destiny. He would be a Shaw specialist, one of those rare actors who are thought of first whenever a director is casting a Shaw play.

And it nearly happened. In 1954, having been through the war in the Combined Services Entertainments, and come out with an even greater passion for the stage, he finally began to make headway as an actor.

He was cast in a television version of Shaw's *Misalliance*, those being the days when television actually broadcast plays instead of 'reality' shows. It was rehearsed in a real theatre, the Stoll in the West End. Although it has long since been demolished, and replaced with a block of flats, it occupied the site that is now another theatre, the New London, where *Cats* was born and ran for 21 years (see 'Cameron Mackintosh and *Salad Days*').

Misalliance was broadcast on 27 July 1954, and on 28 July he was offered a good part in a forthcoming production of *St Joan*, starring Siobhan McKenna, at the Arts Theatre. At last, the fulfilment of a lifetime's dream – Shaw in the West End!

He played the Dauphin, in whose name Joan raises her army for France and against the occupying English, and by whom she is eventually betrayed. Williams, who looked even younger than he was (he was 28), had a suitably short, medieval-looking haircut from Charlie, a rare case of father and son working together.

Kenneth Williams was, in fact, a good actor, and perfectly capable of playing straight parts. The play began rehearsals in August and opened on 29 September 1954. It gave Kenneth a chance to show what he could do with a really good stage role, and the critics loved him. He was on his way.

In the Epilogue to *St Joan*, the Dauphin ages to an old man, and the performance was seen by Tony Hancock's radio producer, Dennis Main Wilson. It was this ability to play a very young man and then change his voice to that of an old one that so impressed Wilson and was the deciding factor when he asked Williams to become a regular on *Hancock's Half Hour*.

St Joan had had a dual effect for Kenneth: it confirmed him as a classical actor but it also made him a star, which effectively precluded a career as a classical actor. Once he was launched on the popular path to fame and fortune, it ruled out his return to the dramatic roles that he most wanted to play and that gave him most satisfaction.

The rest was not just history but tragedy, too, as Kenneth headed into stardom and a never-ending outrageous and camp performance from which he felt he could never escape. He was the master of the sexual and lavatorial innuendo, the 'nudge, nudge, wink, wink' joke, the entire vocabulary of arch expostulations and mock-surprised expressions that made his comedy persona unique. He was brave – there were jokes that today seem tame but in their time took terrible risks with the public taste – and fearless.

Nobody today would raise an eyebrow if a flagrantly homosexual character appeared on radio and television – indeed there are gay characters in all the soap operas and even *The Archers* – but Kenneth Williams did it first. He was a pathfinder and opened many doors for other gay actors (and never has the description been more inappropriate, for Kenneth was far from gay) and writers who wanted to explore the taboos of sexual behaviour. His popularity made it possible for him to say and do much that before him would have been unacceptable, if not arrestable.

There was always darkness lurking within him, which eventually overcame him – his last diary entry, before his death from a drug overdose on 15 April 1988, spoke of terrible pain in his back and his stomach, and asked 'What's the bloody point?'

The prospect of yet another operation, allied to chronic back pain that was at that time incurable, finally pushed him over the edge. His diaries speak of his private pain and reveal the man behind the public persona. He often wrote of his inability to resist the temptation to camp it up, whether on television or in restaurants or at private houses, even with his closest friends. And the sad truth is that Williams was trapped behind the grotesque mask that he had created. Though it earned him a good living, which, after the death of his mother he rarely spent, it warped him into a private prison from which he was unable to escape.

In realising his dream of becoming a star, the best thing that could possibly happen to any actor, he had become his own worst nightmare, a phoney personality that he was unable to shed, afraid that he would find there was nothing beneath it. The kind of work he wanted to do never came his way again, except for one radio play shortly before his death in which he showed, for the last time, that he was a fine actor who could have been a great actor if only he hadn't succumbed to the temptation to speak the several hundred profitable innuendos that were his populist stock in trade.

KENNETH TYNAN AND LOOK BACK IN ANGER

LONDON, 1956

On 8 May 1956, the traditional first-night fashionable audience of a new play by an unknown playwright were bored and appalled in equal measure. The play was being staged at George Devine's Royal Court Theatre in Sloane Square – a playhouse that was a left-wing outpost in the heart of Chelsea, opposite Peter Jones's, the high altar of a class and culture that the play noisily despised. Most theatre critics hated the play, and John Gielgud, seeing it for the first time, thought it 'dreary with no great merit'. No one expected it to be a hit, least of all its author, who was then a struggling young writer living on a houseboat on the Thames – not in Chelsea, but in the far less fashionable Chiswick.

The play, *Look Back in Anger*, was the original 'kitchen-sink' drama, and was about Jimmy Porter, the first of a generation known as 'angry young men'. Porter was very angry – with his wife, with England, with Life. Its three acts tell of Jimmy (played on this occasion by Kenneth Haigh), his wife Alison (Mary Ure), and their friend Cliff (Alan Bates), arguing, reading the Sunday papers and doing the weekly ironing. Marriage has turned Alison into a resentful drudge and Jimmy into a misogynistic bully, while Cliff's constant needling and Alison's friend Helena's interference drive them to ever greater invective.

Jimmy's rants (and this playwright, John Osborne, was to prove the master of rants, on and off stage, in the course of his career) were the last thing most theatre audiences, for whom theatrical people and places were invariably 'nice', expected to see.

Look Back in Anger had been written in two and a half weeks and sent to a wide range of theatrical agents, most of whom were less than impressed. The play seemed destined for a merciful release and a quick death, never to be seen or heard again, the fate that usually befalls first plays by young playwrights. But not this time.

The man who saved *Look Back in Anger* and identified it as a major change of direction for the English-speaking theatre was the drama critic of the *Observer*, Kenneth Tynan, still for us critics what Tom Stoppard called him at the memorial following his early death in 1980: 'the luck of our generation'.

Regular readers of the *Observer* were either avid for, or horrified by, their weekly fix of Kenneth Tynan's theatre criticism. Many older readers dreaded it, especially those who expected a critic to give a well-bred description of their night at the theatre, preferably conjuring up not just the events on stage, along with an idea of whether or not they were worth shelling out a few pounds to see, but, ideally, a suggestion as to the price and quality of the gin at the bar, along with a few witty and well-chosen words about the other members of the audience – a cross between arts coverage and social anthropology.

With Tynan's arrival at the *Observer* those expectations changed and it's a remarkable indictment of British theatre criticism and the rest of us that he remains by far the best-known theatre critic of the second half of the twentieth century. No one else has come anywhere near Tynan's reputation, style, commitment, passion or sheer readability.

With Tynan what you got was not just a thrilling account of what it was like to see a particular play but a passionate description of why that play mattered. And, if it didn't matter, why that was the case and what might have been done about it. For Tynan theatre itself mattered, and in its service (and his own) he raised theatre criticism to the level of an art, making it, as it were, the military wing of the Provisional Playwrights' Front. He wore his left-wing politics proudly, as a badge of what he stood for, the first critic ever to believe that he should announce his own prejudices so that the reader could evaluate what his reviews were about. And it was with his review, in May 1956, of John Osborne's *Look Back in Anger* that the whole face, and direction, of twentieth-century British theatre changed. For ever.

The review was an impassioned one, and made those who hadn't seen the play want to go straight to Sloane Square, while those who had seen it (such as Gielgud) were, amazingly, persuaded to give it another try. Tynan began with his own 'angry young man' swipe, this time at Somerset Maugham, whom he dismissed as an out-of-touch old man saying only what he thought people would agree with. Of Maugham's blimpish and reactionary view of modern, 'state-aided' university students as all 'scum', he said, 'Those who share [Maugham's view] had better stay well away from John Osborne's *Look Back in Anger*, which is all scum and a mile wide . . .'

Far from finding young Jimmy Porter a wastrel whippersnapper who needs a good job, if not a good hiding (punishment was an activity Tynan knew a good deal about, having been very open about his own sexual pleasures), Tynan considers him a modern-day Hamlet:

> Jimmy Porter is the completest young pup in our literature since Hamlet, Prince of Denmark . . . Mr Osborne's picture of a certain kind of modern marriage is hilariously accurate: he shows us two attractive young animals engaged in competitive martyrdom, each with its teeth sunk deep in the other's neck, and each reluctant to break the clinch for fear of bleeding to death . . .

The review finds Osborne's and the play's left-leaning politics a refreshing change from the usual apolitical or nostalgically right-wing fare on offer in most London theatres. And Tynan then delivers possibly the most extraordinary line ever written by a theatre critic and certainly the most famous review line ever: 'I doubt if I could love anyone who did not wish to see *Look Back in Anger.*' Compared with that, the final sentence – 'It is the best young play of its decade' – seems positively tame.

The significance of *Look Back in Anger* was not called into question till much later, when Kenneth Branagh played Jimmy in a 1989 Shaftesbury Avenue revival, which exposed the play's blatant misogyny and told us as much about Tynan as it did about Osborne. It is *not* a great play, as Tynan told us it was, but it *was* a great review.

And it was this review that sent Gielgud back to the Royal Court, from which he emerged as a fan, and it launched Osborne's career and immortalised that of Kenneth Tynan. *Look Back In Anger* spawned dozens of other kitchen sink plays and playwrights. After seeing the play, Laurence Olivier (later to be Tynan's boss when he crossed the River – literally and figuratively – to work as dramaturge at the nascent National Theatre) asked John Osborne to write a play for him. This play, *The Entertainer,* about a broken-down variety comic, is probably Osborne's masterpiece.

We're still waiting for the next Ken Tynan.

THE ENTERTAINER

LONDON, 1957

It is rare to be able to place not just the genesis of a role in the theatre but also whom a character or characterisation is based on and where the actor got the idea for his portrayal. One of the few traceable characters was based – in conception and execution – on the comedian Max Miller, one of the most successful variety artists on the English stage in the first half of the twentieth century.

Miller was known as the 'Cheeky Chappie', and his trademark was a florid suit with plus fours, in colours that could be worn only on the stage. The outfit was completed by a white hat, perched at a rakish angle over his well-cut hair. At a time when it was considered raffish for men to wear anything but navy blue or charcoal grey (with black for funerals), his colours alone might have caused trouble, but he was a big man who was tough enough to look after himself, a ladies' man rather than a limp-wristed thesp, and, fixing them with his piercing blue eyes, he never had any problem with the drunker audience members.

Where he did have trouble was over his other trademark – his near-the-knuckle humour.

Max never used four-letter words – he never had to. His patter was so skilfully structured, timed and delivered that the audience finished the last word of the punchline in their heads, before he said it, and would burst out laughing while he feigned astonishment that their minds could be so dirty.

One example was a little poem that ended:

I like the girls who do.
I like the girls who don't.
I hate the girl who says she will and then she says she won't.
But the girl I like best of all, and I think you'll say I'm right,
Is the girl who says she never does but she looks as though she . . .
Here! Behave yourselves!

The most notorious of his jokes, and one that still raises some blushes – and for which he was banned by the BBC – was about how he found himself on a narrow ledge on a mountain. There was room for only one person to walk along it. Suddenly, to his amazement, he turned a corner and found another person walking awkwardly along the ledge towards him. A beautiful, large and very naked woman. 'Well, lady, I really didn't know what to do – whether I should toss myself off or stay and block her passage!'

Max Miller was notoriously mean. Just like Jack Benny, who was his American counterpart, he made almost a profession out of not standing his round of drinks. His excuse was that his stage persona was so friendly, and in the course of his work he met so many members of the public, that if he did buy his share of rounds he'd be permanently drunk and broke.

He had his moments of generosity and, unlike so many stars, preferred them to be anonymous. As a young man he'd suffered from temporary blindness, so, unostentatiously and very quietly, all through his life he gave large sums of money to charities for the blind.

But, despite his legendary meanness, Miller did occasionally buy a round on those late-night after-show train journeys, when he was among friends. He lived in Brighton, where he was born, and took the last train home most nights, in company with the other theatre people who lived in Brighton (see also 'The Last Train to Brighton'). Among these was Laurence Olivier, perhaps the greatest all-round actor of the twentieth century and the first director of the National Theatre.

At first sight, Max Miller and Laurence Olivier seem an ill-assorted pair but they had more in common than would seem obvious. They were both at the top of their respective professions, rich, famous and respected. Both were constantly on the lookout for fresh fields to conquer and new challenges. And they both lived in Brighton and had plenty of opportunity to observe one another.

An unrelated event in 1956 brought the two together theatrically. A young playwright called John Osborne had written *Look Back in Anger*, the first of the 'kitchen sink' dramas that revolutionised the British theatre in the middle of the twentieth century. At first, it had lukewarm to hostile reviews from the critics and was actively disliked by the luminaries who had so far seen it.

Olivier was one of them. He saw the play early in its run and, like John Gielgud, thought it distasteful but, the Sunday after its opening, he read in the *Observer* a rave review by the foremost critic of the day, Kenneth Tynan. Tynan also telephoned him that day and, on hearing that Olivier disliked *Look Back in Anger*, insisted that they go back and see it together to correct Olivier's first impressions. This time, Sir Laurence was so taken with the talent of the playwright that he contacted John Osborne and asked him to write a part for him. (See also 'Kenneth Tynan and *Look Back in Anger*'.)

The resulting play was *The Entertainer* (1957), in which Laurence Olivier played Archie Rice, a failed but talented music hall comic having, in effect, a nervous breakdown on stage. He played him as a much darker, more bitter and far less successful version of Max Miller, for whom he had considerable admiration and whom he had seen many times on stage performing his particular brand of blue but innocent monologues.

Unlike the fictional Archie Rice, Miller was hugely popular and retained his enormous following all his life. But by making him a burnt-out case, though giving him some of Miller's fierce intelligence, Olivier was able to find the core of the character as he never had before in any contemporary play.

Archie Rice is not Max Miller, just as Laurence Olivier was not Archie Rice; but, as sometimes happens when actor and playwright are able to synthesise their intention for a play, they seemed to breathe with the same theatrical magic in Olivier's triumphant performance.

THE TIES THAT BIND . . .

LONDON, 1959

Michael Redgrave was a remarkable actor, a worthy companion to the Big Three of twentieth-century British theatre – Sir Laurence (later Lord) Olivier, Sir John Gielgud and Sir Ralph Richardson.

Kenneth Tynan painted a vivid pen portrait of these challengers for the theatre's heavyweight championship title when he wrote:

> You have to imagine the English stage as a vast chasm, with two great cliffs either side towering above a raging torrent. Olivier gets from side to side in one great animal leap; Gielgud goes over on a tightrope, parasol elegantly held aloft, while down there in the rapids you can just discern Redgrave, swimming frantically against the tide.

A tall and strikingly handsome man, Redgrave was a lifelong bisexual who had a very passionate affair with Edith Evans when they were both at the Old Vic and married Rachel Kempson, but was well known for his homosexual affairs. Indeed, he spent his last night of leave before rejoining his unit in World War Two not with his wife but with Noël Coward. Many of us admired Rachel's long-suffering patience, only to find that she too had an extramarital life, and had several consolatory flings and one long-term affair of her own in the course of her marriage to Michael.

They all got knighthoods eventually. Olivier got his in 1947 but the Queen made Gielgud wait until 1953. Sir John promptly got himself arrested for importuning in a public lavatory (see 'Gielgud's Rhodesian *Richard II*'), whereupon 1950s Britain was scandalised and the royals decided that the next time a leading light of the British stage was to be knighted he must be safely married and able to line up the wife and children for the photograph outside the Palace. The man they chose had indeed a photogenic actress wife, Rachel Kempson, and three beautiful acting children, Vanessa, Corin and Lynn. Michael Redgrave was assuredly a family man but one whose family also included his live-in male lover.

Redgrave got his richly deserved knighthood but, oddly, his lover was not invited to the Palace for tea. Gielgud, who knew of Redgrave's penchant for bondage, greeted him warmly when they accidentally passed each other in the street not long after Redgrave's honour had been announced, 'Ah!' he cried. 'Sir Michael Redgrave, I'll be bound!'

THE 'RING OF TRUTH' FOR
DAVID TOMLINSON

SAVOY THEATRE, 1959

David Tomlinson, who is today best remembered for his role as the father in the 1960s film version of *Mary Poppins*, starring Julie Andrews, was an actor of considerable stage experience. It was while he was playing in a comedy/drama at the Savoy Theatre in London in 1959, a major West End success, that he finally resolved a comedy/drama in his own life. *The Ring of Truth* was a fashionable play made all the more so by the decision of the then prime minister, Harold Macmillan, to go to see it on the night that he declared that he was calling a general election. This was the 'You've Never Had It So Good' election that the Conservatives won handsomely. With David's own conservative views, it was a success all round.

He had always wanted to be an actor, and, though he thought his father, Charles Tomlinson, an apparently respectable solicitor, might have preferred his son to take a more sedate and stable job, like his own, he was astonished when his father suggested that, as 'Tomlinson' might not sound very dashing, David should adopt a stage name. By now, though, David was a member of Actors' Equity, the actors' union, and a change of name would have set him back in his nascent but burgeoning career. He couldn't understand why his father was so keen for him to use a different surname.

Charles lived with his family in Folkestone at the weekend but, due to pressure of work, lived up in London during the week, not an unusual situation at this time before mobile

112

telephones and email. If there was an emergency, he told his wife simply contact him at his club.

As they grew up, the Tomlinson children – David and his brother, Peter – gradually became aware that there was something fishy about their father's living arrangements, but they couldn't quite put their finger on what it was, even though a colleague of their father was prone to dropping none-too-subtle hints to his sons.

Mr Tomlinson went to some lengths, often unintentionally comic, to conceal from his sons that he wasn't living at his club at all. On one occasion he invited them up to 'his' bedroom at the club, where he had made a feeble attempt to distribute domestic items, such as hairbrushes, around the room. This rather backfired when he rang a bell and summoned a steward to the room, to order some drinks for himself and his boys.

'What would you like, sir?' asked the suitably deferential servant.

'Oh, the usual,' bluffed Mr Tomlinson.

'And what would that be, sir?' replied the steward, shattering Mr T's little act.

It was Peter, then living in South Africa, who finally precipitated the discovery. Peter was travelling to Heathrow by bus (having come over to see his brother at the Savoy), when he happened to look in at the window of one of a row of houses in Chiswick that the bus was passing. There, curtains open, sitting up in a double bed, was his father with a respectable-looking middle-aged woman Peter had never seen before.

That was it. Peter telephoned David from the airport. David looked up 'Tomlinson' in the London phone book. There was a Chiswick number. The telephone was answered by a servant. He asked for Mrs Tomlinson.

'She's out,' he was told. 'Is that Mr Charles?'

'No,' David replied.

'Oh, you sound so much like Mr Charles!'

The game, which had lasted for some thirty years, was up. Charles and his 'second' wife, Sophie, had seven children during their time together. They had a family life, only on weekdays, which produced sons- and daughters-in-law, grandchildren and a set of hobbies and pastimes of which Florence Tomlinson, in Folkestone, had never even suspected – a complete double life.

David's half-brother and his wife, to whom David had spoken when he had called Chiswick, were invited to see *The Ring of Truth* at the Savoy. When they did, David was astonished to see how closely his half-brother resembled old photographs of his father, in World War One uniform, and was even more surprised to hear that the half-brother had six siblings. Not only was this a risky double life their father led, it was also a very expensive one.

When asked why he hadn't wanted David to use the family name, Charles blustered that he didn't think 'Tomlinson' interesting enough for an actor. In fact, he didn't want any one of his family in the public eye – as it might lead to an accidental discovery of the fact that he had more children than his friends and colleagues knew about, in two homes, with two women.

Now the secret was out, David felt hugely relieved, and could not help but reflect, as he made up for the theatre the following evening, how much stranger life often was than any play could ever be.

REX HARRISON LOSES HIS RAG

THEATRE ROYAL, DRURY LANE, LATE 1950s

Rex Harrison was not a nice man. He was rude, irascible, unfriendly and difficult to work with. He had been at RADA with my father, Robert, and they had not liked each other, although, as their first professional engagement, in a play by George Bernard Shaw, Pa's favourite playwright, he played Rex's father.

Many years later, when they were both stars, Pa and I were in the Burlington Arcade, looking for Christmas presents for our wives. The previous evening, on live television, I had organised with Eamonn Andrews an episode of *This is Your Life* for Pa, bringing my brother and sister back from Australia, where they lived, and importing wonderful people such as the director John Huston and Peter Ustinov to celebrate my father's life. It had been quite an evening.

We bumped, literally, into Rex. 'Well, Robert,' he greeted my father, 'I saw you on television last night. Very impressive. Of course, I, with so many wives, Rachel [Roberts] and Carole [Landis]'s suicides, so many divorces, couldn't possibly do *This is Your Life*. But you, Robert' (at this point Rex was gesturing with his impeccable handmade gloves), 'you've had such a different life. I mean, one wife, one family' – he barely glanced at me – 'one house' (here he paused as if looking for another compliment) 'and, of course, one performance. Happy Christmas.'

With which insult, he turned on his handmade heels and stalked off down the Burlington Arcade, leaving us wishing that we could have been quick enough to remember Noël Coward's comment about Rex: 'If that man weren't the best light comedian of his generation he would be fit only for selling second-hand cars in Great Portland Street.'

We needn't have worried. It was Stanley Holloway, his great co-star, who played Dolittle in Rex's biggest hit, *My Fair Lady*, at Drury Lane, who produced, with lightning speed, one of the greatest putdowns ever.

Rex's fans were, naturally, unaware of his bad temper, although it was famous backstage and in theatrical circles. On one memorable occasion it backfired on him. Emerging from the stage door of Drury Lane into driving rain, he was in a foul mood, and simply pushed past the assorted fans who had waited, patiently, for their hero to emerge and autograph their programmes for them.

He brusquely ignored one little old lady who had politely gestured to him with pen and programme, and she was so annoyed at this – the very opposite of what she had expected from his urbane public image – that she whacked him on the shoulder of his well-cut overcoat. Stanley Holloway saw all this from just outside the stage door. As Harrison bent to get into his chauffeur-driven car, Holloway, who had a big voice, having the two best numbers in the show – 'Get Me to the Church on Time' and 'With a Little Bit of Luck' – bellowed, 'Rex! Stop! Stop!'

As Rex paused, then turned round to see what the matter was, Holloway said, loudly enough for the fans to hear (and for their benefit), 'Rex, tonight you've made theatre history. No, you've made world history. Yes, tonight, thanks to your rudeness, for the first time in the whole of recorded history . . . the fan has hit the shit!'

I've always thought that this wonderful piece of impromptu wit was the culmination of an entire cast and crew walking on eggshells for months to make Rex Harrison happy. And failing. Everything to do with *My Fair Lady* had to be moulded to the bad-tempered star's requirements. Even the title.

Shaw's own original title was out of the question. *Pygmalion* was the name of the stone statue brought to life by her sculptor in the Ancient Greek myth, the story that first inspired Shaw to write his play about a cockney girl, brought to upper-class life by learning to speak 'proper'. But it was clear that if the producers of the musical wanted Rex Harrison, and they did, there could be no title that indicated that the most important character was female. They couldn't, for instance, call the show *Eliza* or Rex would walk. Lerner and Loewe came up with *My Fair Lady*, and it was a title of genius, describing the girl but seeing her from the point of view of Professor Higgins – at the forefront and in charge.

Rex Harrison was born to play Henry Higgins and he was memorable as its undoubted star. Who could forget his rendition of 'I've Grown Accustomed to Her Face', that gentle, lyrical love song disguised as a matter-of-fact announcement of the formation of a slightly inconvenient habit? Behind the scenes, however, Rex was closer in character to the tetchier song 'Why Can't a Woman Be More Like a Man?'.

And he was just as difficult a star to live with. I once asked one of the many wives who had left him – Elizabeth Harris, now married to Jonathan Aitken – to sum up Rex in one sentence. 'Well,' she said, clearly able to do so in one word but too polite, 'he was the kind of man who would send back the wine not just in restaurants but in his own home.'

FRANKIE HOWERD'S FUNNY THING

STRAND THEATRE, 1963

London's love affair with the musicals of Stephen Sondheim has flourished in the last ten years or so, but it goes back a lot further – even if it was, then, still inclined to be at the courtship phase.

Sondheim's most popular work over here is, these days at least, *Sweeney Todd*, a very dark take on the traditional story of the Demon Barber of Fleet Street, but the musical that wowed Londoners back in the 1960s (and was to do so again some forty years later at the National Theatre) was a rollicking comedy. The first song made that clear – 'Comedy Tonight' – and the title told the audience they were in for fun, too: *A Funny Thing Happened on the Way to the Forum*.

What's surprising about the history of this transatlantic triumph is that the man who made its transfer from the States such a hit, in the flamboyant, showy role of Pseudolus, the slave, was a performer prone to ill health and depression, and with a stuttering, cheeky-but-cautious, knowing-but-nerdy public persona that seems a million miles from the pizzazz of Sondheim's *A Funny Thing* . . .

This opened in New York in May 1962, and was a smash hit. Would it perform as well in London? And who could possibly match (no one could *replace*) the star, Zero Mostel? The answer was suggested by, of all people, Sir John Gielgud, who was working in New York at the time, to Richard Pilbrow and Hal Prince, who were to present the musical in London. The man they needed, he told them, was Frankie Howerd.

118

Howerd was, essentially, a stand-up comic from the old music hall tradition, and was inspired casting. Pilbrow and Prince flew to London and went to Coventry to see him star in another traditional British form of entertainment: the pantomime. In this case it was *Puss in Boots*.

Having seen him in action on stage, they were entranced, went to the stage door after the performance and offered him the role there and then.

In May 1963, Howerd flew to New York to see Zero Mostel play the part – something not every actor would have done: some prefer not to see anyone else in the role, on the grounds that they might, subconsciously, end up giving an impersonation rather than an interpretation of the part. Howerd wasn't daunted at all, but there was an unfortunate moment, in the first half, when the eagle-eyed Mostel, naturally curious as to what Howerd would make of the show in general and his performance as the slave, Pseudolus, in particular, saw that Howerd frequently had a hand over his mouth, apparently trying to stifle a yawn.

'He hates it! I can't believe the guy! He's bored!' complained Mostel, until he was calmed down by one of the production team, who told him that this was one of Howerd's eccentricities: whenever he laughed he nervously covered his mouth. What had seemed like boredom was in fact enormous enjoyment. After that, all went well, the two men met and got on well, and Howerd flew back to London for rehearsals in August.

The production was directed by the legendary Broadway director George Abbott, who was then 76 and, astonishingly, went on to live for another 31 years, dying at the age of 107. Howerd was nervous of Abbott, who had an austere, not to say distant, way of directing rehearsals, and distant proved to be the operative word when he announced, after the dress rehearsal, that he wouldn't be at the Strand on the opening night as, his work now done, he was flying back to the United States.

Despite the inevitable first-night nerves, made worse by chronic back pain (not helped when Abbott, in a rare gesture of warmth, slapped him heartily on the back), Howerd had a huge personal success as Pseudolus, and the production, which opened at the Strand Theatre on 3 October 1963, was to last through the summer of 1965, a highly respectable run in the days when (with the exception of *The Mousetrap*) a twenty-year life (*Les Misérables*, *Cats*, *Phantom of the Opera*) was unheard of.

Howerd, like all too many great comics (and he was, undoubtedly, great) was in private life a melancholic – he had to be literally pushed onto stage on the first night and was so shaken with nerves after the curtain call that he locked himself in his dressing room for about a quarter of an hour immediately afterwards, before he could bring himself to see anyone. But with *A Funny Thing Happened on the Way to the Forum* he had an unqualified success and, as with his other public performances, gave a huge amount of pleasure to the public.

Today he tends to be thought of largely in terms of the *Carry On* films, or some televised one-man shows, but he deserves to be recalled as a live performer who, in addition to all his other achievements, had the successful launching of a West End hit under his belt. No, not *below* the belt, Missus . . .

THE BIG MATCH: MAGGIE SMITH VERSUS LAURENCE OLIVIER

CHICHESTER AND LONDON, 1964

There are, as Dame Judi Dench once said of her best friend, 'no flies on Maggie'. Dame Maggie Smith – one of the few actresses like Dame Judi whose names outside a theatre are guaranteed to fill it, no matter what they are playing – is formidable. Where Dame Judi gets her way with sweetness and professionalism, Dame Maggie gets hers with massive intelligence and razor-sharp instincts. Her talent was clear, even when she was an Oxford schoolgirl, and she had none of the struggles of a starting actress. Laurence Olivier chose her, very early in her career, to work with him and his National Theatre, both at Chichester and the Old Vic.

Olivier, unlike most other senior members of the profession, could and did surround himself with the finest young talent available. This didn't, however, stop him from being occasionally jealous, and often wary of them, and no young actor or actress was left in any doubt as to who the real star of the show was. Most were deferential and grateful. Not Maggie.

Maggie Smith may have been a comic genius, but she was sharp and combative as well, and, despite the difference in their ages and their respective places in the theatre hierarchy, she refused to be browbeaten by Olivier, as the plethora of theatre stories prove.

The first clash came when she played Desdemona to his Othello. Many Desdemonas are relatively demure, fluffy little things whom almost anyone would be tempted to strangle. Not

121

Maggie's. Hers was a cool, intelligent, sexual young woman who knew precisely what she wanted – a big black warrior – and didn't care whom she shocked (including her father) to get him.

Othello was the last great Shakespearean role that Olivier had not yet played and, although today no white actor would play the title role because of racial sensitivities, in 1964 an actor of Olivier's stature could have played Desdemona if he had chosen to without anyone's batting an eyelash.

Olivier was famous for his use of physical disguises to change his appearance and help create the character he was playing – as with the long nose and black wig that distinguished his Richard III back in the 1950s or the blond hairdo he adopted for the film of *Hamlet* in 1948.

For *Othello* he was forced to go even further, but, as always, he took things to extremes. Having honed his body in a gym, he was covered all over, and I mean *all* over, with three coats of blue-black makeup in a process that took three hours, and his dresser buffed him up to a shine before he went on stage. Presumably because he didn't want any of this to come off in Desdemona's arms, he insisted that she keep her hands off him, to which Maggie replied, incredulously, 'I've come all the way from Venice to Cyprus to see you, you've won the war, I'm pleased to see you – what do you want me to do, back away in f***ing horror?'

Her spunk was construed as insubordination and Olivier, looking for an area where he could best her, took her to task over her pronunciation. She should talk more like a lady, he told her, 'instead of that rather common way you have of speaking'.

The next evening Maggie timed her entrance perfectly until he was made up but not yet dressed. She put her head round Olivier's dressing room door without knocking. There he was – naked, magnificent, and dark as night. 'Howww, Nowww, browwwn, cowww!' mouthed Maggie. Olivier proved her match on this occasion. 'That's *much* better, Maggie, darling,' he said.

On another occasion, when they were on stage, he really lost his temper with her. She had upset him, off stage, by refusing to agree to appear in a Thornton Wilder play with him, so when it came to the scene where Othello strikes Desdemona with a proclamation that he has just received – to which she replies, 'I have not deserved this' – he chose to belt her not with the parchment, but with his hand, sending her crashing to the ground in a crumpled heap.

The rows didn't stop even after the opening on 23 April 1964, Shakespeare's 400th birthday, when they were a tremendous hit. Maggie chose to wear a dress that was longer than usual and more than once she appeared on stage dragging several unwanted cigarette ends with her from the dressing room corridor in her hem. This upset Olivier, who seemed to think this was some sort of plot by Maggie to annoy him. She wouldn't have the dress length altered, so in the end he had to ban smoking in the corridors.

Things didn't improve when she was cast as Hilde in the National's production of Ibsen's *The Master Builder* at the Old Vic, directed by Peter Wood. Michael Redgrave had been cast as Solness, but Sir Michael was showing the first signs of the Parkinson's disease that was to cripple him and bring his career to a premature end. Unfortunately, it was assumed, by the public and his colleagues on stage, that Redgrave's inability to memorise his lines and his sometimes rather slurred speech were due to drink rather than disease.

Olivier, who had been in two minds about employing Redgrave in the first place, was furious, while Maggie, who was acting with a man who kept jumping from one speech (and act) to another, somehow kept the production going until the curtain came down.

There was an appalling scene in the dressing room as Olivier tore into Redgrave and took over the role of Solness on tour. When the production returned to London, he gave some of her performances as Hilde to his new wife, Joan Plowright.

But his secret insecurity about playing opposite someone so talented, so spirited and so young got the better of him, and Robert Stephens, the other half of the most glamorous theatre couple of the late 1960s and early 1970s (see 'Robert Stephens in *The Royal Hunt of the Sun*'), told Maggie's biographer that

Olivier came into her dressing room one evening after the performance while she was chatting with Stephens, and said, 'Oh, by the way, I understand that one of the critics says that you almost act me off the stage. If I may say so, darling angel, in the second act you almost bored me off the stage, you were so slow.'

Revenge is sweet, and the following night Maggie answered her cues so immediately, and so quickly, that Olivier became completely flustered, fluffed his lines, and gave his worst performance in the role. His response was to tell Stephens that he would never work with Maggie Smith again. He never did.

ROBERT STEPHENS IN THE ROYAL HUNT OF THE SUN

OLD VIC, 1964

The British have always avoided exoticism, even in the theatre, and today's stars try with all their might to seem like ordinary people. There were few takers for exotic parts in the sixties and early seventies, and young classical actors wanted Hamlet or Romeo rather than Tamburlaine or Troilus. Robert Stephens was different. He was a daring actor who would try anything, and a director's dream. No risk was too great and he seemed to have none of the English actor's fear of making a fool of himself.

He was married to Maggie Smith and together they were the golden couple of their time, just as the Oliviers had been thirty years earlier. They were to split up, though, before she became Dame Maggie, and Stephens, a couple of years before he died, far too young, in 1995, became Sir Robert. Their son, a glorious combination of the looks and talents of both parents, is the actor, Toby Stephens.

Robert's knighthood was an acknowledgment of his late flowering in great Shakespearean roles, such as Falstaff and King Lear, but he should have been recognised, some thirty years earlier, when he played the sixteenth-century Inca emperor Atahuallpa, in Peter Shaffer's play, *The Royal Hunt of the Sun*. Looking like some great exotic bird, this was his greatest challenge and his finest triumph.

The play, first performed by Olivier's National Theatre company at the Old Vic in 1964, was to be Peter Shaffer's

125

most epic play, and he went on to write several other hits that include *Equus* (1973), *Amadeus* (1979) and *Lettice and Lovage* (1987).

The Royal Hunt of the Sun is based on a historical event – the conquest of the Inca Kingdom in what is now Peru by a few hundred Spanish soldiers, led by the ruthless Francisco Pizarro. At its core is a meditation on honour and trust, and the cultural differences between the warring factions in which the king found it impossible to believe that all men were not bound by honour as his own were. It is also a discussion of racism, a word that was not in use when *The Royal Hunt of the Sun* was written. Pizarro's men see the Incas, a greatly civilised people, as savages and feel no need to treat them as they might treat Europeans.

Atahuallpa, the Inca emperor, goes unarmed to talk with the Spaniards who, breaking a truce, take him prisoner. Pizarro's men then agree to release him if a vast tribute of gold is brought to them. The ransom is brought and, once again, the Spaniards break their word. This time, instead of releasing the emperor, they murder him with the permission of their Catholic priests, subjecting him to a terrible death.

Shaffer had written a superb piece of theatre, both in the almost literally dazzling representation on stage of an exotic and now vanished civilisation, and also by creating what Stephens, in his 1995 autobiography (*Knight Errant*) describes as 'a sort of love story' in the unlikely and deeply moving relationship between the two men – the emperor and his conqueror, Pizarro.

In *The Royal Hunt of the Sun*, Pizarro comes to wonder whether Atahuallpa, who believes he is the incarnation of the Sun God, really might have supernatural powers. He tells Pizarro, with every confidence, that, if he is killed by his captors, then the moment the first rays of the sun touch his body in the morning he will be restored to life.

This of course has parallels in the Christian story of the Resurrection, and is seen as blasphemy as well as nonsense by the priests who have accompanied Pizarro with the intention of converting Peru to Christianity.

Shaffer's Pizarro engages in an enthralling debate with these priests, and trumps their bloodthirsty and vindictive desire to kill this heathen ruler by asking whether their Christ would have had him strangled too.

When considering how the emperor should look and sound, Stephens decided to take a leaf out of Olivier's *Othello* book, when Olivier painted himself from top to toe, worked out furiously in the gym and was marvellously dressed. Stephens literally changed the shape of his body for Atahuallpa, and his makeup and costumes were exotic and otherworldly. A striking portrait of Stephens as Atahuallpa and his friend Colin Blakely as Pizarro was taken by that great stage photographer, Angus McBean, in 1964, and shows Stephens as a wonderfully elegant and exotic character, hair swept back and with eye makeup not unlike that of Elizabeth Taylor as Cleopatra.

As no one really knew what the Inca language sounded like and therefore what sort of accent Stephens should use, he made up his own birdlike way of speaking, with a highly effective and strangely haunting result. Judging by the slight swipe he takes at Peter Shaffer in his autobiography – 'whatever Peter Shaffer may claim now, I had to make it all up' – there was some post-opening jostling for credit re Stephens's interpretation, but there was certainly no debate over the fact that it was he who came up with the movement that, along with the voice, made his Atahuallpa so haunting: 'With my Aztec profile, swept back hair and curious balletic movement, I was hardly surprised when one critic said that I reminded him of Margot Fonteyn, though I've always thought that I looked rather more like Maria Callas!'

What is undeniable, and as the McBean portrait shows, is that he looked (in the best sense of the word) extraordinary, and his performance quite rightly turned him from a good actor into a major player. Atahuallpa may not have risen back to life when touched by sunlight, but playing Atahuallpa in the spotlights of the Old Vic certainly raised Robert Stephens to the exalted ranks of true stardom.

His decision to go for the exotic had worked.

NO LADIES ALLOWED . . .

DUBLIN, 1965

In early 1965, I was one of the hosts of a BBC2 programme called *Late Night Line-Up*, while simultaneously writing a biography of Noël Coward.

Noël had told me that, in his early days as a child actor, his two closest friends were Gertie Lawrence and another child actor, Alfred Willmore. If I could find him, Noël said, I'd learn everything I needed to know about their shared theatrical childhood.

Gertrude Lawrence had died some twenty years earlier. Sadly, Willmore had completely disappeared. I tried hard to locate him. I advertised in all the newspapers for anyone who might know of his whereabouts but to no avail. Finally, I concluded that he must have been one of the millions who perished in World War One, as he would have been about the right age.

I was sent by the BBC as part of my day job, to interview the great man of the Irish theatre, Micheál MacLiammóir, for a *Late Night Line-Up* special. MacLiammóir was the most Irish man I ever met. His brogue was impenetrable and it took me a while to understand the answers to the questions I had come to Dublin to ask. I began with the obvious, 'What', I asked him, 'was your start in the theatre?'

'I was born Alfred Willmore,' came the astonishing reply, 'in the East End of London.' Completely inadvertently, after searching for him for months, I had found him and, with him, Noël's childhood as well as his own. Master Alfred Willmore had been one of the leading child actors in Edwardian London, acting alongside two other such prodigies, Master Noël Coward and Miss Gertrude Lawrence, in *The Goldfish*.

He began his career only a relatively few years after Oscar Wilde was imprisoned for homosexuality. Impressed by Wilde's children's stories, but aware that the author was the subject of some nameless disgrace, he once plucked up the courage to ask his father what exactly all the fuss was about. 'Well,' said Mr Willmore, 'the trouble with Oscar Wilde was that he wanted to turn boys into girls.'

Poor Mr Willmore. His own son, while a highly successful actor and a close friend of those other two child stars, became so obviously homosexual that England, with its restrictive laws, was no longer safe for him. He fled to Ireland, where his flamboyant figure was a leading influence on the twentieth-century Irish theatre scene for many years, as actor and theatre owner.

With his long-term partner Hilton Edwards, he formed a powerful double act on and off stage, and together they ran the Gate, one of the two great theatres of Dublin. The Abbey is the other. The Gate was known for classical Wildean plays, the Abbey for its promotion of all things rural, modern and above all Irish, so the two establishments were affectionately known, in theatrical circles, as Sodom and Begorrah!

Despite this, Dublin was a far less worldly place than London, and it was still a staunchly Roman Catholic city, so even there MacLiammóir had a brush with the law. The testimony he presented was comically incriminating rather than helpful. Still, those were gentler and kinder times.

MacLiammóir found himself up before a jury on an indecency charge. A guilty verdict would, for all that Dublin was a warm and welcoming place, have meant social and professional ruin. An acquittal would place the incident firmly in the footnotes of history and he could get on with far more important things – such as running the Gate. And being more discreet in future.

After he had declared himself not guilty, the whole case fundamentally came down to a question of his word – and his character. Was this beautifully dressed and equally well-spoken gentleman, a pillar of the Dublin theatrical establishment, really likely to be doing unmentionable things in public places?

The jury heard all sorts of testimony to the probity of his character, the strength of his morals, his many kindnesses and so forth, but these were all tributes from his peers, from people for whom he had done favours, or whom he might employ in the future.

What he needed, his defence counsel thought, was someone earthy, someone of the people, a good, no-nonsense, God-fearing and preferably, under the circumstances, female member of the Irish working classes, someone who could recognise a real gent if she saw one. Did, counsel wondered, MacLiammóir have anyone whose testimony might therefore be helpful?

I can't help feeling that, when MacLiammóir said he did, and gave her name, there was a twinkle in his eye and visible signs of his tongue in his cheek. For the good lady called to the witness stand as the last, trump card in persuading the jury of MacLiammóir's innocence was his landlady, with whom he had lodged for some time and who perfectly fitted his defence barrister's profile.

'Mr MacLiammóir? Oh, yes, your honour, I know him very well. Stayed with me a long time, he has. He's a gentleman of utterly good character, your worship. He's been with me quite a while now, and you know, in all that time, he's never *once* tried to take a young lady up to his room!' Mr MacLiammóir was acquitted.

COWARD'S QUICK WIT

SAVOY HOTEL, 1965

While I was researching my (and Noël Coward's) first biography, *A Talent To Amuse*, I was with Noël when he was in his customary suite at the Savoy – his favourite London hotel. There was a knock at the door. 'Enter!' he called. A young man's head popped round the door. 'Oh, Mr Coward, I'm acting with you in your latest film, and I thought I'd introduce myself. My name's Keir Dullea!' 'Keir today, gone tomorrow!' snapped back the Master, and I knew – as if I hadn't already – why he so richly deserved that affectionate nickname. Anyone capable of coming up with a quip like that, as quickly as that, would be an astonishingly good subject for a biography.

By the end of his life, Noël lived at Les Avants in Switzerland and Blue Harbour in Jamaica. He once said to Graham Payn, his partner of many years, whose career he had tried to promote in various musicals in the 1940s and 1950s, that he would like to be buried wherever he happened to die. Death came, quietly and in an impeccably well-mannered way, on 26 March 1973, at Firefly, Noël's favourite home in Jamaica, on his Blue Harbour estate, on a clear, sunny morning – just as he would have wished.

He is buried on a stretch of lawn by Firefly, overlooking the crystal-clear Caribbean waters that he loved so much, and whose paintings of which were yet another side to this extraordinarily multitalented man. True, he couldn't draw figures all that well (there's a hint of Lowry matchstick about many of them) but he captured the sea, sand and sun perfectly, and his grave looks out over them, as he would have wished: the eternal Englishman Abroad.

Which leaves the interesting question of what might have happened if he had passed away in England, at what was in effect his London home – the Savoy. Burying actually in the hotel would have been impossible, and the health-and-safety fanatics would presumably have been less than amused at the idea of scattering his ashes around the hotel suite he used to stay in; but there is the Queen's Chapel of the Savoy, which, far from being a parish church, *is* one of the Queen's chapels, and legally known as a 'royal peculiar'. Given his love of words, his Bohemian private life and his adoration of the royal family, burial there would surely have suited him down to the ground.

JOE ORTON'S DEATH

ISLINGTON, 1967

Joe Orton, the natural successor to Oscar Wilde, was born John Orton in 1933, the product of the welfare state formed during the last years of World War Two. The son of working-class parents in Leicester, he left the dreariness of the postwar early 1950s provincial backwater for London, with a scholarship to Britain's leading drama school, RADA.

Here, in 1951, he met and became the lover of Kenneth Halliwell. Once Joe became famous, people marvelled at the gap between them in wit, creativity, success and good looks and were perplexed as to how they had come together in the first place, let alone maintained a partnership of some sixteen years, but that was to look at the relationship without the benefit of hindsight.

When they met, Halliwell was a slightly older man who acted as a mentor to Orton. He was intelligent, fairly talented, had a macabre sense of humour that appealed to Orton, and though not possessing Orton's pretty-boy looks, was nonetheless attractive – even the photos of them taken on holiday in Morocco in 1967, with their friend Kenneth Williams, show a presentable enough man, if you ignore the toupee (Halliwell went bald at an early age).

Kenneth Halliwell had the benefit of a small private income, and the advantage (for an artist) of having had tragedy in his life. His mother had choked to death in front of his eyes when stung in the mouth by a wasp, and his father had gassed himself at home when Halliwell was 23. These deaths may have kick-

133

started Halliwell's dark take on life, but they wrecked him psychologically.

He and Orton soon moved in together and, after some years, moved in 1959 to Noel Road in Islington, where they lived off Halliwell's private resources plus the dole. Their relationship was always claustrophobic – they lived, slept, worked and played together in one small room, which they decorated with a montage of images from magazines and art books, and entertained themselves by defacing library books. They redesigned the covers to give them a surreal and often sexual twist.

Eventually and inevitably they were caught and sentenced to six months in prison, a punishment that, in contrast to Wilde's jail sentence – which crippled him artistically and financially, and from which he never recovered – was to be the making of Joe Orton. For once, he was alone, away from Kenneth Halliwell, and the change released his imagination and enabled him to find his own voice.

For most of their time together, all through the 1950s and well into the 1960s, they had tried to break into the publishing world, jointly writing gay-themed novels loosely modelled on the Edwardian excesses of Ronald Firbank, in a distinctly Wildean tone.

These efforts failed to get them published, though they did manage to catch the initial interest of Charles Monteith, then a senior figure at Faber and Faber, one of the most intellectually distinguished publishing houses in London.

Monteith had discovered William Golding, whose *The Lord of The Flies* had been turned down by so many others, so Kenneth and Joe (who changed from John for phonetic rather than practical reasons) hoped that Monteith would do the same for them.

Sadly, though, he and another publishing colleague were interested enough to meet them, and to have dinner at the boys' flat – the main course was rice pudding followed by a dessert of rice pudding with jam – the book got no further than the discussion stage, as Monteith, though intrigued, finally judged their work as simply too pornographic for the book-buying public.

Orton's true talent turned out not to be writing novels in tandem with Halliwell, but writing plays on his own. The first to be accepted (in 1963, broadcast in 1964) was *The Ruffian on the Stair*. He found his stage feet with *Entertaining Mr Sloane* (1964), an outrageous (for the times) comedy in which an attractive young thug gets his comeuppance for murdering an old man by being made to live in a *ménage à trois* with the man's equally unappealing sister – and brother. He was taken on by the legendary theatrical agent, Peggy Ramsay, who cleaned him up, mothered him, fed him and sold him as the new bad boy of the English stage.

Entertaining Mr Sloane was followed by *Loot*, which won the *Evening Standard* Drama Award for Best Play of 1966, and by *What the Butler Saw*.

This stage success fundamentally altered the balance of power between Orton and Halliwell, as Joe became the one with the money (much of Kenneth's having been spent over the years they had been together). Halliwell was envious of Joe and frustrated by his own lack of artistic success. He had a few 'exhibitions' of his collages but these tended to be in Soho basements, distant from the Chelsea Bohemian set whose admiration he craved. He became ever more defensive, aggressive, bad tempered and bitter, and Joe, not surprisingly, looked for a way out of the relationship. Aware of this, Halliwell became paranoid about losing him.

Orton wanted and needed to move on – but what to do about Halliwell? Joe talked to friends such as Kenneth Williams about the possibility of buying a house in Brighton, where he could 'park' Kenneth and perhaps just visit at weekends. This clearly wasn't going to work, but it is clear that he still cared about him and didn't want simply to 'drop' him. On the other hand, and equally clearly, Kenneth was holding him back.

Meanwhile, he continued to live the promiscuous life he had always enjoyed, which is graphically described in his diaries. His warmth, sexuality, good looks and generally engaging personality gave him an unerring ability to pick up strangers, driving Halliwell to further extremes of jealousy, until something terrible was bound to happen – and it did.

On 9 August 1967, Kenneth Halliwell murdered Joe Orton. The murder scene was grotesque. It was the bedsit in the Victorian house in Noel Road, Islington – to which they had moved in 1959 – then a relatively sedate and fusty area, a couple of decades away from the centre of fashionable restaurants and politicians' homes that it was to become.

It was a ghastly fate for Orton, poised for greater success with a wider audience, but it was, in a macabre, strange way, a very 'Ortonesque' way to go – a mixture of sex and violence laced with irony. The one thing missing was his trademark wit – there was nothing funny in the fact or manner of his death.

The body of the 33-year-old playwright lay on the bed where he had been sleeping when his head was smashed in by a hammer wielded by his long-term lover. The hammer itself had been placed on Orton's chest in a weird sort of tribute – there was a hint of a royal Egyptian mummy, clutching in death the symbols of authority in life, though in this case the object was not the pen (or more literally the typewriter) that had made Orton famous, but the household implement (or tool – he'd have preferred the latter) that killed him.

Orton's brains, which had made him the funniest playwright of his generation, in a macabre, black-comedy way, were splattered on the wall, where they had been sent with the force of Halliwell's blows.

Halliwell's 41-year-old body lay on the next bed, wigless and smirched with Orton's blood. His own end hadn't added to the gore – he'd taken 22 Nembutal tablets, a barbiturate, washed down with the grapefruit juice from a can that sat on the floor near him.

Unlike Orton, whose body was still warm when it was found, Halliwell had died very quickly – in less than a minute, it was estimated, by the police who were called to the flat by the chauffeur who had come round to collect Orton for a script conference at Twickenham Studios, where he was due to meet with the producer Oscar Lewenstein.

The death robbed Swinging London of its most iconoclastic, and funniest, young playwright, while linking for ever this brilliant successful man, clearly on his way up, and the bitter, damaged and ultimately hopeless lover, mentor and friend who slew him.

Orton was the 'Oscar Wilde of the Welfare State', and in many ways Wilde's natural successor. Unlike Wilde, though, he was determined to put his genius into his work rather than his life. In that he would have succeeded, but, because of the bizarre manner of his death, it is his life rather than his work that remains a source of fascination, and the record of his life, in his diaries, that explains both the fascination in and the motive for Halliwell's murderous assault. As Halliwell's suicide note said, 'If you read his diary all will be explained. KH. PS. Especially the latter part.'

Humour was eventually introduced, however, in the film of Orton's life, called *Prick Up Your Ears* after the well-reviewed and highly readable biography by John Lahr. After the men were (separately) cremated, their ashes were mixed together before being scattered at Golders Green cemetery. In the film, as they are being ladled together, one of Joe's relatives says to the famously acerbic Peggy Ramsay (played by Vanessa Redgrave), 'Oh, dear, I don't think I'm putting an equal amount of them into the jar,' to which Peggy/Vanessa replies, 'It's meant to be a gesture, dear, not a recipe!'

GLADYS COOPER'S SURPRISE BIRTHDAY

LONDON, 1968

Dame Gladys Cooper, my grandmother, despite a stage career than spanned the best part of seventy years, never liked to look back, if she could help it: she was always much more interested in the present and the future.

Partly as a result of this she wasn't all that keen on birthdays, but, when it came to her eightieth, her family agreed that something had to be done.

She was, of course, in a play, *Out of the Question*, with her friends, Michael Denison and Dulcie Gray. In her autobiography, *Looking Forward, Looking Back*, Dulcie recalls how Gladys wasn't known for learning her lines, but somehow got them in the end, and was in any case 'delightfully easy to work with'.

The production was a happy one, marred only by Gladys's irritation at discovering a programme note announcing that 'Dame Gladys' socks are from Marks and Spencer'. She had worn couture clothes all her life and didn't want her fans to think she was somehow letting them down by wearing mass-produced clothing.

Gladys (we in the family always called her 'G') didn't, as we've seen, believe in looking back, only forward – 'getting on' was her watchword. You had to 'get on', no matter what you were getting on with, don't look back, don't stop.

G was the first woman to run a West End theatre, having been the actress/manager of the Playhouse during the 1920s, a remarkable achievement at any time, given that even now female producers are rare and female managers can be counted on the fingers of one hand. My grandfather, Herbert Buckmaster, returned from the Boer War to discover that the chorus girl he had married had turned into an executive with, as he later complained, 'an office and a telephone'. So he promptly divorced her, not because she had been chronically unfaithful, which she had, but because he couldn't imagine being married to an executive with a telephone. They stayed friends, though, through two more marriages each, and towards the end of her life it was he, as the owner of Buck's Club, who gave her opening-night parties.

G was never a great driver, and Dulcie recalls that she hired two handsome young brothers (she still had an eye for a good-looking man) to alternate in driving her back to her home on the banks of the Thames at Henley, enjoying not just their looks but that they drove a sports car that was capable of hitting 120 miles an hour.

I had given up accepting lifts from her myself some years earlier when, sitting in the passenger seat alongside her, I asked if she could possibly slow down a bit, as the speed she was travelling at was clearly worrying other drivers on the same stretch of road, let alone myself. She seemed to ignore me. Finally, I slammed my hand on the dashboard. 'Stop!' I shouted. She stopped, in the middle of the road. 'What is it dear?' she demanded. 'G, I can no longer stand it,' I quavered, still shaking. 'Stand what, dear?' 'Your driving, G.' 'Am I?' she replied, absent-mindedly, from behind the wheel, 'I thought *you* were?'

Anyway, on G's eightieth, we didn't know quite what to do. It was, officially, *Out of the Question* to do anything much about the eightieth birthday – it was thought that G would be furious if she thought anyone knew she was eighty – but my father, Robert Morley, Gladys's son-in-law (my mother was her daughter Joan), was never one to miss the opportunity of a good meal.

On the night itself, the play went ahead as usual, but, unknown to Gladys, all the seats had been secretly booked for her family and friends. The other actors were warned of this, as it was expected that the audience, anticipating the surprise party rather than the play, would be less noisily appreciative of the action on stage than usual. They indeed were, and this rather threw Gladys, who couldn't understand why they were so muted.

In the play her stage grandson has to open the door to a friend. That evening the part of the friend was played by Robert Morley, to his mother-in-law's astonishment. Ever the professional, however, she refrained from showing surprise or recognition, and carried on as if this were always part of the play.

Robert, who had brought on champagne and glasses, gave us all a drink – including G – then went to the front of the stage and said, 'Ladies and gentlemen, tonight is the eightieth birthday of a wonderful woman and a great actress, Dame Gladys Cooper, and I hope you will all join me in celebrating it now!' He then turned to an astonished Gladys and said, 'Tonight the house has been paid for. It's full of your friends and we're now going to stop the play and head off over the road to the Ivy and have dinner!'

At this the audience stood up and cheered. Gladys, with a twinkle in her huge blue eyes, hissed, in a stage whisper, 'Not a paying audience? But I'm on a percentage!' The same ironic sense of humour that kept her going through the occasional dark patches in her life, as well as adding to the pleasure of the happy ones, was evident some years later, too.

When she was dying, in November 1971, still on the road in yet another production of *The Chalk Garden*, she asked me to hand her a mirror. For a moment, the woman who had been the great beauty of World War One, the first woman to have a brand of cosmetics named after her, the woman who had been the pin-up of a million servicemen and the subject of envy for less beautiful women everywhere, studied her face, ravaged by cancer. 'Well, dear,' she announced, 'if this is what cancer does to the cheek bones, I really don't think I shall bother to have it again.'

She died in her sleep that night.

ROBERT MORLEY VERSUS ALAN AYCKBOURN

LYRIC THEATRE, 1970

Several years ago, when the playwright/director Alan Ayckbourn wanted to stage my play, *Noel and Gertie* at his Stephen Joseph Theatre in Scarborough, I (bruised from a recent American production in which the show had been cut, rewritten, even renamed by its star and director) suggested timorously that he might want to produce the show as written.

'*What?*' he thundered, '*You* have the cheek to tell me how to stage your play when your bloody father all but destroyed mine and did it in a way that made me a successful playwright?'

Hard though it is now to believe, after 69 plays and phenomenal success all over the world, there was a time when Ayckbourn, the most prolific and popular British playwright since Shakespeare, was unknown. In September 1969 he was still young – just thirty – and was thrilled to hear that his play, *How the Other Half Loves*, then playing in Leicester, might move into the West End the following year, starring my father, Robert Morley. If it worked, Ayckbourn knew it would make his name and his fortune, which his *Relatively Speaking*, though a critical success in London in 1968, hadn't quite managed.

But he reckoned without Pa's habit of changing the plays in which he appeared and rewriting them to make them his, rather than the playwright's. Alan had started his career in the theatre as a lowly actor, cast in a small part in a Pinter play. He ruefully recalls asking playwright Harold Pinter a question

141

about his character, to be told to 'Mind your own f***ing business!' – so Ayckbourn wasn't used to actors with real power, and expected them to respect the words on the page. He didn't know Pa.

Alan was duly summoned to our family home near Henley to talk about taking the play to Shaftesbury Avenue. Robert announced that there were a number of changes to plot and character than needed to be made to improve the play. At first Alan Ayckbourn bit his lip, but he soon couldn't help interrupting Robert's flow (not easy, that) to object to the wholesale destruction, as he saw it, of his work.

The character Robert was to play, Frank Foster, was a jogger. Not a good one, but a jogger. Robert unsurprisingly thought that, given his rather large girth, it might be less than convincing with him in the role and suggested another hobby for Frank. 'What about flower arranging?' he mused. Alan, who had had enough of keeping quiet and trying to smooth things over, thought not. 'But a lot of men arrange flowers in Japan!' ventured Robert. Alan reminded him that the play was set in the dinner-party belt of Surrey.

And so on, with Robert threatening to drop the idea of the play completely, and Alan calling his bluff. In the end, of the dozen or so major changes suggested by Robert, Alan agreed to three. But Alan's ordeal was just beginning.

Rehearsals began on Pa's birthday, 26 May, and *How the Other Half Loves* opened at the Lyric, Shaftesbury Avenue on 5 August 1970. At an early stage in rehearsals, when Robert was aware of how miserable he was making Alan with his 'improvements', he said to him, 'Mr Ayckbourn, I am going to take this play, and I will make you very unhappy with what I do, but in the process I will also make you very rich.'

And, given the success of the play, Robert was right on both counts. The first night was fun and funny, and the next morning's papers were almost uniformly pleased with it, as were Robert and the rest of the cast. It was a huge hit in the West End and on tour and was quickly snapped up by the Americans after its West End run,. (One tour stop was Nottingham, where, I remember, Robert found, on his dressing room table, a one-word note from the room's previous occupant, Leonard Rossiter: 'Help!')

The only person who wasn't happy was the playwright, Alan Ayckbourn. Alan himself recalled later, 'Robert is an actor who rapidly gets very bored, and, in order to refresh himself and engage himself, he always treats the theatre as one huge game organised by himself. The joy of the man is that he does have great enjoyment for what he does, and infectious, playful enthusiasm. Unfortunately, the people who suffer are the people on stage with him, or who are attempting to get on stage with him . . . So you have a few working actors ploughing doggedly on with their scripts, clutching on to characterisations which Robert delights in bombarding and trying to upset – hiding their props, or locking doors, or jumping at them from cupboards, which tends to make the play look a little ropey . . . in the end I stopped going to see it, as it made me unnecessarily upset when he changed anything . . .'

And change he did, adding one-liners, jokes about the Common Market and numerous bits of 'business'. The fact that Ayckbourn didn't come to see the play after a while upset Robert, but even there the two men were at cross-purposes: when Robert said it would be nice for Alan to come to the theatre, he didn't mean to sit in on the show and then give the actors notes, but to pop round to the dressing room for a drink. Given that Alan felt physically sick with what Robert was doing to his play, it was an invitation that he had little difficulty in resisting.

This was, however, one case where there was a happy ending, and Alan Ayckbourn has always been gracious enough to record that Robert played his part in making it so. Given what he did with Alan's script, it is only poetic justice to let Mr Ayckbourn have the final word:

I learnt one great lesson from Robert, which was that you can't argue with the system. Eighty per cent of that audience had paid to see Robert Morley, and I, as an unknown dramatist, had really no right to interfere with that process if I wanted to take the money. If I could have suffocated Robert to the extent of preventing him from doing his own thing, I would actually have offended many of the punters who, because of him, were coming to see my play.

SIR ROBERT HELPMANN AND THE UMPIRE'S HUT...

AUSTRALIA, 1970s

Sir Robert Helpmann was one of the great names of twentieth-century British ballet, and – a rare if not unique double – also an accomplished actor. Born in Australia in 1909, he began dancing professionally in 1927, after studying with Anna Pavlova and members of her company.

He moved to London, joining the Vic-Wells Ballet, the first incarnation of what would eventually become (via the Sadler's Wells Company), the Royal Ballet. Ninette de Valois, spotting his potential in London in the early 1930s, said, 'I can do something with that face.' He was her principal male dancer from 1933 to 1950, and was Margot Fonteyn's first great partner, before ceding that position first to Michael Somes, then, of course, to Rudolf Nureyev. But, long before the young Rudolph Nureyev literally leaped to freedom at Paris airport and defected to the West, Helpmann had moved on to a world that encompassed more than just ballet.

Although he was, later in life, to become first co-director, then the sole director, of the Australian Ballet from 1965 to 1976, he had, from the 1950s onwards, taught himself to be a remarkably talented actor on stage and screen, performing in plays and films, often at the same time as his appearances in the ballet.

He had always admired Shakespeare, and was to appear many times at Stratford-on-Avon and at the Old Vic. Indeed, two years after staging and dancing his own ballet version of *Hamlet*, he was playing the Prince of Denmark in Shakespeare's

145

version, repeating his performance again on consecutive nights in 1948, the only performer ever to do both.

In later life, after he had relocated to Australia, although he had a full-time job at the Ballet, he would often take out tours of Shakespearean productions in which he starred. His favourite was *The Tempest*, which at one point he hoped to film.

Well past his physical prime, he nonetheless continued to radiate an air of theatricality and had great authority on stage. Off stage, he had huge energy and his ballet training had left him in terrific physical condition. Many observers made the mistake of thinking that his fey personality and almost proto-homosexual flamboyance meant that he was just an adorable clown. He was not. He was one of the great men of the international theatre in two completely different, if related, fields during the first half of the twentieth century.

Helpmann loved the art of makeup, was proud of his ability to become, with a few sticks of greasepaint, either an old woman or a prince, and was, unsurprisingly, given the length and breadth of his career, very good at it.

He was wildly (and unapologetically) camp, and, when he died in 1986, his obituaries were among the first to give a frank account of their subject's sexuality and presentation, and he would, I think, have been proud that they showed the way for other homosexual men to be so openly described.

So the love of makeup both expressed and emphasised one aspect of his personality while being an essential part of his stage career. And it was this pride in doing his own makeup, to his own highly exacting standards, that led to my favourite Robert Helpmann anecdote (although there are many), and it happened during one of his last tours.

He had taken his beloved Shakespeare, in the best traditions of Victorian and Edwardian actor-managers, from one theatre to another, gradually seeking out the smaller playhouses after he had conquered all the large and obvious ones. This determination to go, as it were, further and further afield in order to reach new audiences led to his performing at some very small, and sometimes rather *ad hoc* venues.

On one such occasion, he was performing Prospero, his

favourite role, at a cricket club. There were no functioning lights in the dressing room so he disappeared, shortly before he was due on stage, to finish his makeup.

As the curtain-up time got closer and closer and no sign was seen of Helpmann, a young assistant stage manager (ASM) was sent to find him. Which he eventually did. There he was, in the umpires' hut, balanced precariously on a chair, which he had placed on a table, under a naked light bulb dangling from the wooden ceiling, makeup stick in one hand and a tiny mirror in the other.

'Oh, Sir Robert!' the ASM called out. 'Do be careful! Are you sure you're all right!' 'Of course I am, dear,' he replied. 'I've made up in worse places than this before. But what really worries me, is . . . how do the umpires manage?'

PETER O'TOOLE'S MACBETH

OLD VIC, 1980

The history of the theatre is littered with stories of unknowns who 'went out there an understudy and came back a star' (to quote the musical *42nd Street*) and others about disastrous miscalculations by major productions and big stars. The truth is that there are very few of these. More often, big-star productions work and understudies often have their moment of glory in front of their mother and their agent, and then return to knitting in the dressing room. One exception occurred on 3 September 1980.

It was one of the most heralded London opening nights in years. It was the flagship production of the season of plays put on by the new management of the Old Vic, that most historical and prestigious of theatres, then newly headed by actor-manager Timothy West. The play was *Macbeth*, and the actor, the star, playing the title role was Peter O'Toole.

O'Toole's reputation was primarily as a film star – his *Lawrence of Arabia* was one of the great screen performances of the century – but his roots and his love were in the live theatre, and the audience was avid to see one of this country's highest-profile actors back on stage for the first time in five years, in one of the great Shakespearean roles.

His popularity was in part based on his well-publicised hell-raising, a man with a taste for flamboyance and the high life, and the combination of bravura private life and dazzling screen and stage chemistry meant that the Old Vic was packed with an eager audience.

148

Adding to the excitement, there was also a hint of blood in the water and the sharks were gathering, fuelled by the amorphous but entirely credible 'word on the street' that was leaking out from the rehearsals. Backstage, Timothy West was known to be unhappy with the way director Bryan Forbes and actor Peter O'Toole were handling the play – and had indeed written to them to say so. Rehearsals, said the gossip via most of the actors and backstage staff, had not gone well. We theatre critics then present had all heard something of the conflicts but, then, we had heard all this before and often they were smoothed out by opening night and no cause for concern.

Not this time. This time the rumours turned out to be tamer than the reality. Neither the production nor the performance had come right in rehearsals, and there was a barely suppressed hint of panic in the air.

The traditional 'curse of *Macbeth*' seemed to be rampant and was haunting the cast, despite O'Toole's best effort to avoid ill fortune by referring to it as 'Harry Lauder' and his Lady Macbeth, Frances Tomelty, being addressed by him as 'Lady Lauder.'

There were too many accidents and alarums. 'Lady Lauder' had come off her motorbike at over seventy miles an hour, nearly killing herself; the actress playing the first witch was briefly hospitalised with a burst appendix; O'Toole himself narrowly avoided death in a car accident. And then there was the spooky coincidence that Lilian Baylis, the greatest figure in the Old Vic's illustrious history, had died of a heart attack on the first night of *Macbeth* in 1937.

Princess Margaret, a great supporter of the arts and an admirer of O'Toole, had heard of the backstage troubles and gamely agreed to attend rehearsals. She announced to the cast, in her inimitable voice, 'I was born in Glamis and I've come to take the curse off it.' Sadly, despite the legendary healing powers of the medieval monarchy, the twentieth-century variety seemed unable to work its magic.

The opening night was worse, far worse, than can have been expected. Laughter greeted the three witches in the opening scene – referred to by one critic as being more modern

Knightsbridge than medieval Scotland – and it went downhill from there. Jack Tinker, in the *Daily Mail*, thanked O'Toole for having given him such a uniquely merry evening, and the rest of the press corps laid into the production as a whole, and into O'Toole in particular.

The Times thought that

His walk is an exhausted lunge, his voice thick, hoarse and full of abrupt sledgehammer emphases . . . His verse speaking consists of a heavy lurch from beat to beat, delivered in measured, sustained tone, and depending on prolonged phrasing within a single breath. Arresting to begin with, if only as total departure from modern verse convention, it grows extremely monotonous and blots out the sense.

The *Sunday Times* referred to

the premeditated awfulness of O'Toole's performance . . . this Macbeth stemmed from an utterly private conception of personal glory, a conception so intense that it rejected any offer of help or advice in its realisation, a conception that spurned the company and spurned the audience.

As for me, I didn't think it was nearly as bad as my colleagues seemed to think – it was far, far worse.

The final word must go to Jack Tinker, however: 'It is Hollywood at its most hilarious self parody. The voice is pure Bette Davis in her *Baby Jane* mood; the manner is Vincent Price hamming up a Hammer horror.' It was a disaster.

Timothy West publicly denounced the production the next day, after which director Bryan Forbes took to the stage the following night, after the curtain calls, to denounce (without naming him) West's public statement, comparing him (by implication) to Judas Iscariot. The public was thrilled, watching not just a theatrical disaster but a theatre company tearing itself to shreds.

Waylaid outside the stage door on that same second evening,

as he was going into the theatre to get ready for the performance, Peter O'Toole was asked by the television crews what he made of the press coverage of the previous night's performance. 'Pretty hairy!' he smiled, putting on as brave a face as he could.

As he left the theatre a man turned to his wife, 'Well, after that, all I can say is I hope the dog hasn't been sick in the car!' That seemed to sum up the general view. But, just as a motorway pile-up attracts crowds of onlookers, so O'Toole's *Macbeth* drew in the fans, making it a box-office success even if it was a dramatic (in both senses of the word) crash.

Most of the laughter was reserved for the extraordinary sight of him staggering onto the stage with a couple of daggers in his hands, his head and body literally dripping with fake blood and gore, then announcing, after not so much a Pinteresque pause as a Peteresque one, 'I have done the deed' – surely the most superfluous sentence uttered in a theatre that year.

And yet, and yet . . . O'Toole's interpretation may have been very . . . individual, shall we say, but it was valid. It was just that it was about eighty years out of date. This was the first year of the 1980s, there was a sense of change, of a new decade, even though naturally no one knew what was going to happen – the Falklands, Mrs Thatcher's three terms in office, the collapse of the Berlin Wall and of communism in Eastern Europe. But there was nonetheless a sense of a fresh start, from the new Prime Minister in Downing Street to the New Romantic pop movement.

And here was Peter O'Toole giving a superb impersonation of an Edwardian actor-manager, all graphic stage effects (and gallons of blood), and, in grand declamatory style, savouring every Shakespearean phrase. The slowness was one of the main faults found with his delivery and the pace of the production, but it was inherent to the style of his performance, in which everything in the play was savoured rather than rushed.

True, Brian Blessed as Banquo's ghost, also drenched in blood, was understandably found funny by the audience, but that was not the inevitable reaction. Once people had read the reviews they came not to praise Caesar (or in this case

Macbeth) nor to bury him, but to laugh at him. And they did so even when there was nothing really to laugh at, because it had become fashionable to do so, because they thought they should. The emperor's new clothes were in fact worn by the audience rather than the actors: O'Toole, far from wearing nothing, was swathed in the long overcoat and astrakhan collar of an Edwardian actor-manager and, had he been taken at face value and on his own terms, it would have been a distinctly unfashionable but interesting, and artistically valid, interpretation.

As it was, he laughed that bark-like, ironic, worldly laugh of his all the way to the bank, as the crowds continued to queue at the box office (this was before Internet booking, after all) and the Old Vic bars took record profits. It was a typically unlucky *Macbeth* in many ways, but not in terms of financial return.

It took a while for O'Toole to return to the stage once the run of Macbeth ended, some four months later, and when he did so it was to triumph in the West End run of *Jeffrey Bernard is Unwell*. But that's another story . . .

HELLO, DOLLY!

PRINCE OF WALES THEATRE, 1982

'Well, hello, Dolly . . .'

One of the great anthems of showbiz boomed out on the stage of the Prince of Wales Theatre in London's West End in 1982, as the star of *Hello, Dolly!* appeared, glittering in diamonds and swathed in fur, wearing an outrageous wig and a dazzling smile.

The show had already been a box-office hit in Birmingham before transferring to the West End, and now it was setting a record. Not because of the box-office takings (great though they were), nor for the length of run (it was a bit early for that) but because this was (and remains) the first time in West End history that this major musical about the matchmaker Dolly Levi was starring – a man.

The man, of course, was Danny La Rue, who as he himself once said, 'I'm not a star, darling, I'm a f***ing legend!'

How did he get here and what was he doing? It was certainly a strange tale, and one that was unlikely to have happened had it not been for the unique combination of interwar Irish poverty and the showbiz opportunities opened to a generation of performers by, bizarrely enough, national service during World War Two.

La Rue had been born Danny Carroll in Cork, Ireland, on 26 July 1927 (he changed his name after World War Two because La Rue sounded sexier and more exotic). His family moved to England when he was young, settling in the cosmopolitan enclave of Soho. Danny was to be an altar boy at Soho Square's Roman Catholic Church, St Patrick's.

153

He would say to a Dublin audience, when he returned as the world's most famous female impersonator, 'Look what the English did to me! I left Ireland in short trousers and I've come back in a frock!'

He began his working life as a window dresser, swiftly moving onward and upward, staging small-scale fashion shows, and appearing, in the evenings, in nightclubs such as Winston's and its rival, Churchill's, where he gathered an ever-increasing audience.

His nightclub act was born of his time in the navy, which he joined during World War Two. He was part of the entertainment corps, which, lacking women in the ranks, had to use men to take the parts of the girls. This wartime experience of dressing up in drag was almost universal, stretching from the deep-jungle concert parties that *Privates on Parade* was to recall, to prisoner-of-war camps where the prettier, younger prisoners (lieutenants in particular) played the female roles.

There's something really very British in all this, and it doesn't really have anything to do with sexual orientation – although the French would probably disagree. It has, instead, a lot to do with the uniquely British tradition of having young men play female roles on stage. (This was the norm in Shakespeare's day, for instance, when all his leading ladies were teenage boys.)

The huge number of men, including our very own Danny Carroll, who found themselves in uniform, among audiences needing entertainment, meant that a great many of them ended up playing women's roles on stage, or in makeshift entertainments areas in locations as varied as Colditz Castle and the jungles of the Far East.

After hostilities ended there remained a short, and to today's mind extraordinary, public taste for large-scale shows featuring soldiers and ex-soldiers in drag. This passed away (mercifully) after a couple of years, but by now Danny La Rue had developed not just a taste but an astonishing talent as a female impersonator – a description he vastly prefers to 'drag star'.

La Rue made an amazingly convincing, and beautiful, woman, the effect being emphasised by his catchphrase,

'Wotcha, mates!' delivered in a deep, gruff voice, and by his invariable habit of appearing at the end of the show, for the farewell number, as himself, dressed therefore as a man.

After starting with appearances in clubs owned by other people, in 1964 he graduated to one of his own, Danny's, in Hanover Square. This swiftly became one of the most fashionable clubs in the West End, and his act was not only very convincing, it was also very funny – combining old-fashioned British 'sauce' with surprisingly accurate and entertaining satire on leading politicians and figures from the arts and social world. One of his colleagues at Danny's was Ronnie Corbett, and the sight of the two of them as Rudolph Nureyev and Margot Fonteyn (and I think you can guess which one was the ballerina) regularly brought the house down.

It also brought the *beau monde* in, with Nureyev one of the visitors, along with the likes of Princess Margaret and Lord Snowdon.

Hello, Dolly! followed various spectacular one-man shows and in a way was La Rue's apotheosis. True, he had been voted Entertainer of the Decade in 1979 but to star, in a female role, in a major musical such as Jerry Herman's *Hello, Dolly!*, and to be taken seriously while doing so, was an astonishing achievement.

Alongside his nightclub work, his shows (one at the Palace being particularly successful) and *Hello, Dolly!*, he has also been a regular pantomime dame since the 1960s, when he worked in panto for the producer Tom Arnold. Now pushing eighty, he continues to appear not just in panto but in music hall, where he was for many years a mainstay of the BBC television show *The Good Old Days*.

He may no longer fill massive West End theatres as he did in his heyday – the only two seats vacant in his West End show in 1969 were those reserved for Judy Garland, on the day that she died – but he still gives pleasure to audiences throughout the country, a one-man phenomenon maintaining a tradition that stretches back to Shakespeare. And, even though he's now rather more mumsy than Marlene, the title song of *Hello, Dolly!* still (mildly altered) suits him well: 'You're still looking swell, Danny, we can tell, Danny!' Long may he do so.

BURTON AND TAYLOR IN PRIVATE LIVES

LUNT-FONTANNE THEATER, BROADWAY, 1983

It was the theatrical sure thing: a great play, tried and true, a Broadway audience desperate enough for a star vehicle that they were willing to invest a record-breaking $2 million in advance bookings, and two of the world's most famous actors in the leading roles.

He was a ruggedly handsome stage and screen actor with a fabulous voice, as famous for his Shakespearean theatre appearances as for his action-adventure movies. She was not only an Oscar-winning film star but acknowledged to be one of the great beauties of the century. Between them there was a back-history that even the most imaginative studio publicist couldn't have invented.

They had met on the set of *Cleopatra*, one of the most troubled movies ever made, in which she was playing the irresistible queen of the title and he was the virile and sexy Mark Antony. Sparks flew between them from the very first day on the set and, despite her many on-again, off-again illnesses and the inconvenient fact that they were both married (she to the popular singer, Eddie Fisher, he to his long-time wife, Sybil), they were soon embroiled in a highly publicised affair that caused two divorces and their subsequent marriage to each other.

But the path of true love almost never runs smooth, and, while they were, and remained, literally mad for each other, these two spoiled and selfish stars found themselves able to live neither with nor without each other. When they were together they fought, screamed, insulted each other, their break-ups (often fuelled by alcohol) as tempestuous as their reconciliations; when apart, they were miserable, wretched and lonely. They survived and destroyed not just one turbulent, passionate, diamond-strewn marriage to each other (1964–74), but another (1975–6), both ending in spectacular divorces.

Coincidentally, the play they chose some years after their second divorce to revive their flagging careers was about . . . a glamorous divorced couple who cannot live together or apart, a self-absorbed duo who re-meet several years after their divorce and realise they are meant for each other, only to have another blazing row.

The stars? Richard Burton and Elizabeth Taylor. The play? Noël Coward's *Private Lives*. The reunion was irresistible box office – two of the icons of the 1960s together again, on stage, this time in a play that exactly reflected their own tempestuous and all too notorious history.

It was as close to a sure thing as a theatrical producer could imagine. It couldn't miss. Or could it?

There was clearly nothing wrong with *Private Lives*, which still today qualifies as one of the best light comedies (with a dark streak that gives it that vital extra bite) ever written. Noël Coward had originally written it in a scant five days as a vehicle for himself and his best friend and muse since childhood, Gertrude Lawrence. They opened in 1930 at the Phoenix Theatre in London, where it was a massive sell-out from its first night, through the London run and on to another standing-room-only run on Broadway.

Coward and Lawrence had a personal and professional magic that made *Private Lives* magical too – as well as being witty, worldly and, by the standards of the early 1930s, rather shocking in its cynicism. And yet the cynicism was laced with a defiant romanticism, a refusal to accept the restrictions and regrets of the everyday realities that eventually wear down and emasculate even the greatest passions. Together, Noël and Gertie made an impossibly glamorous pair.

The big question before opening night was whether Burton and Taylor would display similar charisma as Elyot and

157

Amanda. We knew that they were both capable of giving strong stage performances – Burton mesmerisingly so. But we also knew that both were well past their romantic sell-by dates. True, they were film rather than stage actors and the strain of eight shows a week would be a heavy burden for a duo who were older and more tired than their ages (she 51, and a victim of too many illnesses; he 58 and a raddled wreck of a man still fighting an unequal battle with a whisky bottle) would suggest.

Yet it's undeniable that both still had star power, a sort of glow that distinguishes them from the merely beautiful or talented or lucky. And, though the two lead characters are meant to be in their late twenties, they had so often been (and still are) played by much older (because starrier) actors. The hope here was that the public would be interested not only in a new production of the play, but also in two living legends on stage, in what was thought to be a fictionalised version of their own relationship.

They opened on 8 May 1983, twenty years after their heyday, and closed, ignominiously, after a couple of months before going on a distinctly underwhelming tour, which ended, as have so many other dreams, in Los Angeles.

Critics and audiences alike found the Burton and Taylor combination had run out of steam. What went wrong? Neither ever seemed to have learned either lines or Coward's complicated verbal rhythms. Worse, the passion that had been the hallmark of their real-life relationship wholly failed to ignite on stage, and they reserved their fire for their constant offstage rows. Burton, rightly or wrongly, gave the impression of being half drunk and both looked for the entire run as though they would prefer to be somewhere, anywhere, but in the Lunt-Fontanne Theater.

It is now clear, with the benefit of hindsight, that neither Burton nor Taylor was remotely a Coward character, and their coming together in *Private Lives* late in their careers was a commercial rather than a cultural decision. Theatre is a medium of passion, and, despite their history, it was clear to all of us unfortunate enough to witness it that their performances lacked that vital chemical component that raises it above the pedestrian. True, they had known Coward offstage for many years, and Burton had a signed photo of Sir Noël, plus a photo of himself with Noël and Elizabeth Taylor, in his dressing room for the duration of the run. However, neither was of Coward's theatrical world, and – despite their own on- and offstage relationship and the superficial similarities to their story – neither remotely resembled the personality of either Elyot or Amanda.

The disappointment was palpable and was reflected in the play's short run. They limped on for as long as the advance held out but there were no further bookings and, of course, they did not work or even see one another again. Two months later Burton married Sally Hart thus eliminating even the most avid fan's hope of a reconciliation.

A year later, a more final curtain was to descend when Richard Burton, happily married and beginning to enjoy an acting renaissance with a chilling performance opposite John Hurt in the film of George Orwell's *1984*, suffered a cerebral haemorrhage on 5 August 1984, in Switzerland and died. It was the end to one of the most celebrated relationships of the twentieth century, but the sad truth was that the relationship's magic pull on the world – and especially for the two people involved – had already died, in the Lunt-Fontanne Theater on Broadway.

ANTONY SHER'S RICHARD III

LONDON, 1984

The South African actor, Antony Sher, has made his career in Britain for many years. As talented a writer as he is an actor, he has written novels, memoirs and plays, none perhaps as moving as *Primo*, his own adaptation of Primo Levi's Auschwitz diary, *I, A Man*, which he played in London and subsequently in New York, with admirable restraint, to deserved acclaim. It was, incidentally, the only time in my experience that a great performance has been greeted by a rapt, and frequently tearful, audience, with total and respectful silence, their applause seeming somehow frivolous in view of the material they had just seen.

But that performance was wholly his own. Of the many outstanding performances for his home company, the Royal Shakespeare, and the National, he may always be remembered for taking on a role associated with someone else and making it uniquely his own. He won an Olivier Award for it, in 1984, and that award encapsulated his dilemma because the role is, has been, and, it seemed, always would be Laurence Oliver's, no matter who else played it.

The part was that of Richard III (in Shakespeare's play of that name), the wicked, crippled king who destroys everyone between him and the Crown, and on the way murders children, women, relatives and friends, as well as enemies. Richard is a gift to a clever actor and each new interpretation allows for new insight into the psychology of evil. The effect of his withered arm and leg on his self-loathing, the rapid wooing of his sister-

160

in-law after he has killed her husband, the brilliance of Shakespeare's lines in Richard's mouth – all of these combine to make him one of the most exciting characters in theatrical literature.

Olivier took on Henry V as the great role of his youth, but it was Richard III, whom he first played in 1944 at the Old Vic, far more than the gentle Hamlet, who fired his mature imagination. And, for decades following his first foray into the part, another Richard was unthinkable, especially after the 1956 film version. Indeed, his playing of the part has been frequently parodied, on stage and in film, and is immediately recognisable: the stilted, rather reedy voice and delivery, the sense of mischief playing about the lips, the shuffling, slightly sideways gait, the dropped shoulder, and all the other props and mannerisms of a definitive performance that seemed to have a label on it saying, 'Don't even *think* of parking here.'

Eventually, in 1984, Antony Sher took it on, and took it over, and the sovereignty of the role was forcibly ceded by Olivier, who was still alive at the time. Sher must surely have had at the back of his mind Olivier's comment to another actor who had tried the part after him: 'Very good, my boy, very good indeed. But the part's still mine!'

Nobody understands this better than Antony Sher himself, who later wrote, in his autobiography:

Now is the winter of our discontent. You don't even like to say it. Don't like to hold it in your mouth. It's been in someone else's. His. You can taste his spit. Feel his bite marks round the edges. His poised, staccato delivery is imprinted on the line: 'Now. Is the wintah. Of our. Discon-tent.'

Once cast in the role at the RSC, to which he has been linked for many years, he had to find a way to approach Richard that was not an imitation of Olivier. Physically, he achieved it with one of Olivier's own favourite solutions, props and disguise. His brainwave was to use a pair of crutches with elbow-height arm rests and grips, which seemed to give him four legs. The long medieval sleeves that he wore in the role added to this effect, making him look (especially when he scuttled around the stage on the crutches) like some monstrous spider.

As well as providing a radical new interpretation of a role that had risked being preserved in aspic, Sher also wrote about the whole experience, from initial discussion to first night, in *The Year of the King*, a stage diary that gives a fascinating glimpse into the process of putting on a classic Shakespeare play.

Here Sher recalls the results that using crutches brought him:

> The wing span (Richard's reach) is enormous and threatening. The range of movement is endless: dancing backward like a spider, sideways like a crab. And you can cover distances very swiftly with a sweeping, scooping action, almost like rowing, the polio-afflicted legs dragging along underneath . . .

The result wowed the critics and public alike – the reviews were so enthusiastic that Michael Caine asked Sher whether he'd written them himself – and provided the major performance in a classical role that every stage actor needs as a crowning glory to a distinguished career.

The Queen rewarded Sher with a knighthood in 2000, a royal tribute to his wicked king. But as he took the curtain call each evening after Richard's final despairing cry of 'a horse, a horse, my kingdom for a horse!' he could surely hear Olivier begging for his role back: 'Very good, my boy, very good indeed. But the part's still mine!' And now he could answer, truthfully, 'No, sir, not any more.'

MICHAEL CRAWFORD IN THE PHANTOM OF THE OPERA

HER MAJESTY'S THEATRE, 1986

When Michael Crawford created the title role in *The Phantom of the Opera* at the musical's opening on 9 October 1986, at Her Majesty's Theatre, London, his prosthetic makeup took more than two hours to apply and thirty minutes to take off. Half of his face had to be movie-star handsome, the other, which was covered by a mask until the final dénouement when Christine (played originally by Sarah Brightman) tears it from his face and reveals his disfigurement, had to be grotesque. Given the huge amount of makeup that Crawford had to wear, he asked for a bit of a prosthetic nose job so that his exposed half-face could look even more romantic in contrast to the deformity revealed when Christine tears it off. The makeup took months to develop, trial and error governing the amalgamation of greasepaint, plastic, rubber and specially made cosmetics. Every night his face had to be moisturised and closely shaved and the prosthetics fitted, before two wigs, two radio mikes and two contact lenses (one white and one clouded) were emplaced. And then he had to be able to sing in it.

The musical was one of the biggest hits of all time and even now, two decades years later, there are queues every night outside Her Majesty's for tickets to add to the total sales of more than $3.2 billion. *Phantom* is a phenomenon. It is also an industry. It has been seen by more than 100 million people worldwide in hundreds of cities in more than twenty countries including the UK, the US, New Zealand, Japan, Austria,

163

Canada, Sweden, Germany, Brazil, Mexico, Australia, Holland, Switzerland, Belgium, Korea, Denmark, Spain and Russia. There are 130 cast, crew and orchestra members directly involved in each performance. It opened at the Majestic Theatre in New York on 9 January 1988 and ran there for seventeen years.

The original-cast album of the *Phantom of the Opera* was the first in British musical history to enter the music charts at number one. Album sales now exceed 40 million worldwide and it is the biggest-selling cast album of all time. The show was conceived as a rock opera on the lines of Andrew Lloyd Webber's earlier hit with Tim Rice, *Jesus Christ Superstar*, but in the course of researching and writing the score Lloyd Webber came to see the show as far more romantic – and ultimately more in keeping with the Victorian period in which the action is set. He saw his then wife, Sarah Brightman, for whom he wrote the show, as a coloratura soprano and, for her voice, a different kind of music was required.

The show has won more than fifty major theatre awards including three Oliviers, the most recent being the 2002 Oliver Audience Award for Most Popular Show, an *Evening Standard* Award, seven Tony Awards including Best Musical, seven Drama Desk Awards and three Outer Critic Circle Awards.

Each performance requires 230 costumes, 14 dressers, 120 automated cues, 22 scene changes, 281 candles, 250kg of dry ice and 10 fog and smoke machines. The dazzling replica of the Paris Opera House chandelier is made up of 6,000 beads and weighs one ton. It took five people four weeks to build it. For the drapes, 2,230 metres of fabric were used, 900 of them specially dyed. The tasselled fringes measure 226 metres. They are made up of 250kg of dyed wool interwoven with 5,000 wooden beads imported from India. Each one is handmade and combed through with an Afro comb. When it moves to a new theatre, the touring production needs 27 articulated lorries to transfer the set.

Much of *Phantom*'s initial success was due to the performance of Michael Crawford. But Crawford was by no means the obvious choice as leading man in the musical. Most of us thought of him as a television star, a comic actor of considerable talent, but not as a singer or a romantic antihero with a chandelier for a weapon.

He had starred in the hugely popular 1970s sitcom *Some Mothers Do 'Ave 'Em* and, although he had appeared in the hit stage musical *Barnum* and the movie musical version of the theatre hit *Hello, Dolly!*, with Barbra Streisand, his television success made him an unusual choice for the dramatic and intense Phantom.

My wife was in a Benjamin Britten opera with him when they were both children and knew he could sing. But it's a long way from boy soprano to dramatic tenor and Crawford proved he was up to the job.

The sound that echoed round Her Majesty's during Crawford's time was not so much music as applause. *Phantom* made him a megastar and paved the way for his later, and hugely profitable, career in Las Vegas and as a concert performer all over the United States. Since *Phantom*, he has built a fine career as a performer in stage spectaculars such as *EFX* in Las Vegas, which was a multimillion-dollar show built especially for him.

That applause reflected not just the achievements of Crawford and Brightman, but the talents of designer Maria Bjornson and director Hal Prince, as well as an amazing company and orchestra. The show was a triumph, but, lest we imagine it to have led a charmed life without incident, there was one particularly accident-prone preview when, during the final confrontation scene between the Phantom and Christine, all hell broke loose.

The computer-driven candles had risen through the stage floor as usual, while the hundred-plus trapdoors all over the stage were shut. Michael was about to hurl Sarah across the stage when the computers that run all the set changes went wrong.

All the trapdoors suddenly opened, which meant that not only did he nearly throw her into a hole, but both performers had to avoid gaping spaces in the floor as they carried on singing furiously.

To add to their growing discomfort, the bed from the previous scene, in which the Phantom kidnaps Christine before the eyes and pistols of the *gendarmerie* waiting to seize him, came lurching back on stage, and the organ, which had come on from the wings to decorate the Phantom's lair, now decided to wander off again on its own. Making matters worse, the candles began to go up and down, one of them, on its return journey, going up the gap between Crawford's leg and his trouser leg, effectively trapping him where he was. Then the candle bulb went on, burning his skin as it did so, while all the time he had to act and sing with total concentration on the deeply dramatic scene he was performing.

Finally, after every possible prop seemed to have been hurled on and off the stage (including a portcullis whose descent could have killed either one of them), a stagehand used old-fashioned elbow power to pull the bed back off stage and out of view. And, just as suddenly as it had started, the computer glitch sorted itself out, just in time for the dénouement.

It was always joked backstage that the Queen had awarded Michael his OBE not for services to the theatre but for not running screaming from it on nights like this. Crawford has always been the calmest of actors, professional to a fault, and cool under fire. His health has not been great – he had to leave the cast of Andrew Lloyd Webber's *The Woman In White* because of colitis – but he has always been a rock as well as a workhorse.

The makeup that took a couple of hours to apply now takes the current Phantom a mere forty minutes, thanks to changing makeup techniques. When Crawford in make-up met Joss Ackland on the stair from the dressing room to the stage, he was mortified to find that Ackland immediately recognised him – 'Hello, Michael, how are you?' while Crawford forgot Ackland's name. The irony wasn't lost on either of them and they burst out laughing.

KEN DODD'S BRUSH WITH THE TAX MAN

THE HIGH COURT, LONDON, 1989

Over the years, a number of actors and comedians have run foul of the tax man. My own father, Robert, even had a loophole named after him. Totally innocent, and finally exonerated in court for income tax evasion (he moved us all to America, took the perfectly legal tax break, then decided he didn't like it after all and moved back), Pa was deeply insulted that the Henley tax inspector didn't believe that he really intended to emigrate and took him to court. Ever after, that particular scenario, no longer on the books, alas, has been known as the Morley Loophole.

But some entertainers have been much more eccentric about money and none more so than Ken Dodd. He doesn't trust banks and his eccentricities included hiding high-denomination banknotes into any spare place he could find at home – shoeboxes, the fridge, the larder, holes in the ground – and taking barrowloads of cash to pay into offshore bank accounts without actually declaring any of it. As a result, he ended up, in 1989, in the High Court on trial for tax evasion.

Although Dodd is well on his way to achieving his long-standing ambition of having played *every* theatre in Britain, this must surely have been his least favourite appearance. This was one case when his trademark tickling stick would get him nowhere, and nor would his jokes.

He did, though, have the inestimable advantage of having the late (but then very much alive and kicking) George

Carman QC on his side, the man of whom the comedian Barry Cryer said, 'He'd even get Hitler acquitted!'

This unnerving and deeply unpleasant experience almost immediately found its way into Dodd's comedy routines, which were now peppered with jokes such as, 'Have you read about how it was in Victorian times? When income tax was still three pence in the pound? Trouble is, I thought it still was!' Some of my colleagues insist that Ken Dodd is the funniest man in Britain, a great artist, and one of the few true originals of our time. My friend Michael Billington, the serious long-time drama critic of the *Guardian*, has been known to follow Dodd to appearances all over Britain and finds that his difficulties with the tax authorities have merely enriched his material.

This misfortune aside, he has otherwise enjoyed an extraordinary career, with several hit songs (especially 'Tears', which reached number one in 1965) and his title song, played at the end of every live performance, of 'Happiness'. He consistently breaks the record at whatever theatre he plays, for the longest show at that venue. For example, if they once had a four-hour musical, he makes sure that his-one man show (plus support acts, but still mostly Dodd) lasts four and a quarter hours.

In the High Court, he was not given the choice of how long he could talk. Mr Carman QC ruled the trial with his usual iron discipline. The crucial question was whether Ken Dodd had deliberately perpetrated a criminal act or not. The likelihood was that, if found guilty, he would go to prison. His barrister's defence, his own undoubted eccentricity, and a string of testimonies to his character, his goodness and his charity work (everyone took his talent as self-evident) meant that, though he was forced to pay back hundreds of thousands of pounds in back taxes, he was able to leave the court a free man.

Even the tax man is happy with him now, and it's lucky for his sake that he didn't go to prison. Had he ended up at Wormwood Scrubs the risk is he'd be determined to break even the most hardened old lag's record and would still be in there, cracking jokes to happy inmates, long after his parole was due.

DANIEL DAY-LEWIS AND HAMLET'S GHOST

NATIONAL THEATRE, LONDON, 1989

Sometimes the ghosts are real.

Cecil Day Lewis, novelist and academic, was the Poet Laureate from 1968 until his death, aged 68, in 1972. He was married to Jill Balcon, the actress daughter of film producer Michael Balcon. Their son, Daniel, was only fifteen when his father died, and the loss affected him deeply, although his father had been very ill, on and off, since a series of heart attacks when Daniel was only eight. An introverted and sad boy, Daniel had become a withdrawn and private man and has written, in a posthumous collection of his father's works, of his own frequent melancholy and sense of decay. It is odd, therefore, that he chose to become an actor, odder that he is so good at it, unless you believe, with Alec Guinness, that acting is the best way to hide. Daniel Day-Lewis is, in fact, a great actor, able to subsume his own personality into whatever role he undertakes and he can now pick and choose his projects, which, inevitably, lead to yet more Oscars and other accolades.

He learned his craft in the traditional way, at Bristol Old Vic drama school, scored a major stage success in Julian Mitchell's *Another Country* (which also featured the young Kenneth Branagh and Colin Firth), and starred in two major 1980s films, *A Room With a View* and *My Beautiful Launderette*.

Thus, the announcement of Daniel Day-Lewis as Hamlet, in Richard Eyre's March 1989 production of the eponymous play, at the National Theatre, seemed like dream casting. Because of his other problems, though, it turned into a waking nightmare for the actor.

The reviews were fabulous and the public flocked to see this intense young star giving his best performance to date in the most challenging – and satisfying – role available to a younger actor. And then, on 5 September 1989, with only seven performances left, Day-Lewis walked off the stage during the first act of *Hamlet*, collapsed in a sobbing heap and was unable to go on – that night or for the remaining performances, which were played by his understudy, Jeremy Northam.

What happened? The answer, strangely (in every sense) was that Day-Lewis saw something during the early emotionally charged scene where Hamlet sees his father's ghost: 'Angels and ministers of grace defend us! Be thou a spirit of health or goblin damn'd . . . be thy intents wicked or charitable, thou comest in such a questionable shape that I'll talk with thee . . .' In that scene between grieving son and his recently deceased father, Daniel actually saw the ghost of his own dead father, Cecil Day Lewis, standing on the stage and staring at him. Daniel staggered off the stage, inconsolable, and simply could not carry on.

Day-Lewis has always been known for the intensity with which he prepares for every role: in retrospect having him play a deeply melancholy, disturbed prince who comes close to the madness he feigns, and who is driven to murder by the intensity of loss he feels at his father's premature death and his desire to avenge it, now, with the benefit of hindsight, seems like tempting fate.

That he had a mental breakdown of sorts is undeniable, and, under the circumstances, entirely understandable. No opprobrium attached to him, no ridiculous 'the show must go on', and he received entirely supportive reaction from press and public alike.

But since that night he has remained firmly in the film world, and has been less than complimentary on occasion about the theatre, on the grounds that he feels there's still a certain snobbery about film actors in the theatre world (he may be right), but one hopes that eventually, like Ian Holm after decades away from the stage, he will one day feel confident and committed enough to return to the theatre and give us some of the intense magic that he invariably works on the silver screen.

PETER O'TOOLE IS FAR FROM UNWELL

APOLLO THEATRE, 1989

During the long and extremely successful run of *Jeffrey Bernard is Unwell*, an elderly man with a ruined face sat in the bar and drank solidly through the play almost every night. When the rest of the audience returned to their seats after the interval, he did not. With no obvious signs of drunkenness, he simply drank his way through the play's initial run of two and a half years.

It was hard to believe that once, this man had been famously handsome. Married four times, he had been blessed, as a young man, with movie-star looks, a cross between James Dean, Johnny Depp and Lord Byron, and for his many female admirers one of the most depressing side effects of a lifetime of his drinking (and he had started early) was the way he had turned from dark-haired faun to ravaged old man. His face was lined and haggard, his cheeks – which in early middle age seemed to have expanded like a chipmunk's – not so much sunk as torpedoed.

When I was the theatre critic of the *Spectator*, he wrote the brilliant 'Low Life' in the same magazine, a weekly column once described as 'the longest suicide note in history'. If so, it was also the funniest suicide note in history, as he chronicled a life lived on his own terms, exactly as he wanted to live it. He was a racing man, a ladies' man, a lover of Soho, and a life-long alcoholic from choice, not addiction.

He had few theatrical aspirations, although he had worked briefly as a stagehand – 'Too much like work, old fella' – in order, I think, to bed the largest possible number of actresses. He used to boast about Wendy Richard as one of his conquests, especially after she became famous, first as the sexy Miss Brahms in the sitcom *Are You Being Served?* and now as a long-time regular in *EastEnders*.

Until his friend, Keith Waterhouse, wrote a play about him, he would rarely bother with the theatre, which seemed to him much less exciting than his natural milieu – the racecourse or, more likely, the Coach and Horses pub in Soho, where he spent most of his waking hours. The play, which was based on the 'Low Life' columns, was so funny and contained so many unlikely episodes, such as a cat race, that the fact that they were actually true never occurred to the audience except for those of us who knew him and realised that Keith had in fact had to tone down some of the episodes to make them palatable for a general audience.

In Waterhouse's play, Jeff is accidentally locked into the Coach and Horses for the night and he spends it, inevitably, drinking up the landlord's stock, and conjuring up figures from his past, including past lovers, who hurl at him, again and again, accusations about his life and relationships, which he amiably accepts as being perfectly true.

The question arose concerning who could possibly play a once beautiful wit with a taste for the bottle. Who could create, just by walking on the stage and pointing his own sunken features at the audience, an immediate visual history of Soho bars, early mornings, dustbins and empty bottles, and a bloody good time having been had, so to hell with the physical wreckage involved? Who else, of course, but Peter O'Toole?

O'Toole had exactly the right gangly charm, brilliant on-stage presence, and, perhaps best of all, memories of his own, now lost, unearthly beauty. As Lawrence of Arabia he had been not handsome nor good-looking but beautiful in an entirely masculine way. Noël Coward quipped that, had O'Toole been any prettier in the role, they would have had to rename it *Florence of Arabia*, but the fabulous face had gone by the time the play opened at the Apollo Theatre, Shaftesbury Avenue, in September 1989, destroyed by too much good living and the high life, just like that of the man he was playing.

It was a perfect role for O'Toole, who loved and relished it and brought his real-life equivalent vividly to life. And what of the man himself? The inevitable result of Jeff's drinking was that he was often too drunk or too ill to deliver his weekly article for the *Spectator*. The long-suffering editors who employed him would simply put a line in the space where the copy should have been, which read, tactfully, 'Jeffrey Bernard is unwell'. This made an ideal title for the play that won the 1990 *Evening Standard* Award for Best Comedy.

It played for two and a half years through several casts and theatre moves, and was revived ten years later at the Old Vic with most of the same cast. Its protagonist had sadly died in the interim, in 1997, aged 65, having already lost a leg to the alcohol. Once his liver went the same way there was nowhere to go but into the ground. But, during that first run, he practically lived at the Apollo, thrilled to see the great Peter O'Toole playing him on stage.

He delighted in telling friends, hangers-on and total strangers who happened into the theatre bar that, much as he liked seeing Peter act, the call of the bar was often stronger than the lure of the greasepaint, so he would sit out much of the play there, chatting to the suitably impressed barman.

On one such evening, though, a man who had arrived too late to be shown to his seat wandered into the bar to while away the time. He looked at the man with the collapsed cheeks and red-veined nose propped on a stool, and eventually said to him, 'Don't I know you from somewhere?'

'My name,' he responded, grandly, 'is Jeffrey Bernard.'

'Don't be bloody stupid,' said the man, 'It's a bloody play, isn't it? Jeffrey Bernard's out there on the bloody stage.'

And, of course, they were both right.

VARIETY IS THE SPICE OF LIFE – ISN'T IT?

BUCKINGHAM PALACE, LATE 1980s

It was the end of a long day for Prince Edward, who had returned to Buckingham Palace from the borders of Soho and Covent Garden, where he had been working for Andrew Lloyd Webber, the composer of such hit musicals as *Cats*, *Starlight Express* and *The Phantom of the Opera*.

You can imagine the scene: the Queen and Prince Philip relaxing with a gin and tonic after another busy day of meeting government ministers, dealing with her 'red boxes' (in which government papers are sent to her) and agreeing the details of yet another overseas tour some months in the future. She was pleased that her youngest son had found employment that he enjoyed – though she would have preferred it to have been something more obviously like hard work in the eyes of her subjects and, more to the point, the press. Never one to show her emotions in public, she was perfectly capable of showing them in private, at home, with her family. And today she, like her son, was feeling in need of a rest.

So, when Edward started talking about his day at the office, his visit to the appropriately named Her Majesty's Theatre, where *Phantom* was enjoying a great success, and bemoaning his workload, the Queen was less than sympathetic.

Didn't she realise, the Prince droned on, that theatre was much misunderstood? That it involved great concentration, dedication to duty and a professionalism that most people could only dream about? That, despite the surface glitter and

175

the public glamour, it was incredibly difficult work that involved real hardship and guts to bring off properly?

This was too much for the sovereign to bear. 'Of course, I do, Edward,' she snapped. 'Your father and I are very well aware of how horrendous time in the theatre can be. We have to sit through the Royal Variety Performance – and look as if we're enjoying it!'

MAGGIE SMITH ON BROADWAY

BROADWAY, 1990

'It's true I don't tolerate fools but then they don't tolerate me, so I am spiky. Maybe that's why I'm quite good at playing spiky elderly ladies.' So says Dame Maggie Smith. Dame Maggie qualifies as one of our national treasures, not just for her acting but for her wicked sense of humour, delivered in the trademark drawl that makes even witty lines sound that much funnier.

She often comes up with plenty of one-liners herself, and one of my favourite stories involved the Broadway transfer of Peter Shaffer's West End comedy, *Lettice and Lovage*.

This had premiered in the autumn of 1987 in London, where it was a huge personal success for Maggie, whose over-the-top character perfectly suited her more mannered and stagy techniques: indeed, one critic complained that she gave more of a revue turn than a performance, but that in a sense was the point. Lettice was a larger-then-life character who lived in a sort of theatrical make-believe, and it was precisely because Dame Maggie (who can sometimes do understated, quiet and tragic, but not for long) is so good at creating this sort of creature on stage that the play took off. And full marks also went to Margaret Tyzack for making so much of the other character, Miss Schoen.

Lovage, by the way, refers to an Elizabethan infusion that both of them drink before setting off to wage their personal war on the modern world.

Peter Shaffer is one of those rare British playwrights who are as popular in New York as they are in London – indeed he spends most of his time in New York, so it was natural enough that *Lettice and Lovage* transfer there, in 1990, after the London run.

The show was an immediate hit but audiences and Dame Maggie were distracted by the sounds of an African-American gospel musical playing next door – the two theatres share a wall – during the quietest moments in the *Lettice and Lovage* matinée. The stage manager, who had heard his share of Maggie-Smith-is-a-Holy-Terror stories, simply *had* to find a solution in time for the evening performance. He had to locate some black velvet drapes ('blacks' in theatrical parlance), that were specifically designed to muffle sound, to produce a soundproof barrier between the two theatres. He explained the problem to the stage manager of the adjoining theatre, rushed to the theatrical-supply store, bought and sewed them, and finished arranging them – one set on the rear wall of each playhouse – minutes before the star arrived.

As she entered her dressing room she was met by the exhausted but satisfied stage manager: 'I think you'll be happy, Dame Maggie – we've hung the blacks.' She gave him a sardonic look. 'You've gone much too far!'

JANE HORROCKS IN LITTLE VOICE

COTTESLOE THEATRE, NATIONAL
THEATRE, 1992

When the movie *Little Voice*, starring Michael Caine and Brenda Blethyn, opened in 1998, it had only moderate success. In the long run it was considered worthwhile by the film industry chiefly for newcomer Ewan McGregor's sensitive performance as a gormless electrician, helping a painfully shy girl to find her self-esteem. A few knowledgeable critics pointed out that the movie was an adaptation of a London stage hit called *The Rise and Fall of Little Voice*, but nobody noticed that the play itself had been unique in origin.

It was by Jim Cartwright, a well-known if iconoclastic playwright who had worked the neat trick of writing experimental plays that were then staged by major companies. Indeed, his three most recent plays, including *The Rise and Fall of Little Voice*, had been produced by the National Theatre.

But, unlike all his previous work, this play was the result of a close friendship and background knowledge of its leading player. Cartwright knew that the actress Jane Horrocks, a fine theatre professional but publicly best known as Edina's (Jennifer Saunders) ditzy secretary in *Absolutely Fabulous*, had an extraordinary trick – she could imitate the voices and styles of all the great female singers of the 1940s and 1950s. She could sound exactly like Judy Garland or Ella Fitzgerald and sing their songs with precise attention to intonation and

179

phrasing. Watch her, and it's Jane Horrocks; close your eyes and it's Judy or Ella.

Cartwright decided to write her a play that exploited this extraordinary talent and the result was *The Rise and Fall of Little Voice*, a hilarious and poignant story of a lonely teenager with a vulgar mother whose boyfriend, an opportunistic 'agent', tries to exploit the girl's only talent.

Plays have often been written for individual stars but Horrocks was not, at the time the play opened, a star, although she was a highly competent and experienced actress. It was, therefore, a considerable risk that the National Theatre took in staging this one, except that Cartwright had one more piece of insider knowledge that he knew would stand him in good stead in persuading the National to go forward: Jane Horrocks's partner at the time was the hottest theatre director in London, who was also the artistic director of the highly respected Donmar Warehouse, Sam Mendes.

With Mendes at the helm, and Horrocks doing what only she could do, *The Rise and Fall of Little Voice* opened in the Cottesloe Theatre at the National on 16 June 1992 – and it was a sensation. The supporting cast couldn't be bettered: the versatile Alison Steadman, known for her stage and television success as Beverley in *Abigail's Party*, was perfect as the awful mother, and Pete Postlethwaite, then mainly a stage actor but now known to a wider audience through films such as *Brassed Off* and *The Usual Suspects*, played the horrendous boyfriend. Collectively, they were one of the big hits of the season, transferring first to the Aldwych Theatre in the West End and then to Broadway. It won both the *Evening Standard* and the Olivier awards for Best Comedy, and made Jane Horrocks an above-the-title star.

The only problem, of course, is that Jim Cartwright's play can never be performed again unless another actress can be found with the same uncanny trick. Horrocks is now a major star, and, with two children, is – dare I say it? – unlikely to be mistaken for a sad teenager. But nobody who saw her in *The Rise and Fall of Little Voice* will ever forget the extraordinary sight and sound of Judy Garland's big expressive voice coming out of her forlorn and tiny frame.

JUDE LAW IN THE BATH

LYTTLETON THEATRE, NATIONAL THEATRE, 1994

These days fans and paparazzi alike would give a fortune to see Jude Law naked. Like most stars, however, he knows how to keep covered up and away from prying lenses when not fully clothed. All attractive male stars, just like their female counterparts, are now fair game when it comes to a revealing shot.

But if you hopped in Doctor Who's TARDIS and popped back in time to 1994, you could have seen him stark naked on stage in the Lyttleton, one of the three auditoria that make up the National Theatre in London, where he was playing a fairly minor character in Sean Mathias's production of Cocteau's *Les Parents Terribles*.

The play, set among a strange, Bohemian family in Paris, co-starred Frances de la Tour (Miss Jones in the Seventies sitcom *Rising Damp*), Corin Redgrave (brother of Vanessa) and Sheila Gish.

Law's character, Michael, has an unhealthily close relationship with his mother (Miss Gish) and their onstage behaviour seems more like that of lovers than relations. Eventually (to Mummy's fury), he falls in love with a girl, and, in a deceptively casual but actually highly erotic scene, the curtain goes up on Michael in the bathroom at his girlfriend's flat.

Mathias, a clever director who knew what he was onto here, placed an old-fashioned bath in the middle of the stage, with a naked Jude Law sitting in it. Law got out, chatted to his

181

girlfriend, and towelled himself dry in full view of a (hushed and very concentrated) audience!

At that point Law wasn't a star, let alone the Hollywood heartthrob he has become through films such as *The Talented Mr Ripley*, but he clearly had something special about him, even then – he was the only member of the cast to transfer from London to Broadway.

The play, on Broadway, was renamed *Indiscretions*. In his private life, this international sex symbol, famous for his elfin beauty, has mostly been anything but indiscreet, but, for English and American theatregoers in 1994 and 1995, he was as upfront (literally) and as revealing as any of them could have possibly wished.

SAM WANAMAKER AND SHAKESPEARE'S GLOBE

BANKSIDE, LONDON, 1997

Just after World War Two, a young American made his first visit to England. He came looking for the eternal verities he had fought for – history, continuity, art and culture. He was an actor and his great love was Shakespeare, so, as soon as he arrived, he asked a Londoner to take him to Bankside, to Shakespeare's theatres – the Globe, the Rose – so he could drink in the atmosphere of the Old World and understand what Shakespeare was writing about. He was appalled to discover that no trace existed of either of them.

His name was Sam Wanamaker and, like many Americans, he believed that everything was possible. All it needed, surely, was energy and imagination. An idea began to form, an idea so grand in conception that it could only be a lifetime's preoccupation: why not build a replica of Shakespeare's theatre on the banks of the Thames so that succeeding generations would be able to perform his plays in as close as possible an atmosphere and setting to the original? Wanamaker couldn't see any reason why it couldn't be done.

His plan was to recreate a Shakespearean theatre, built by craftsmen using (to the extent it was possible) the designs, materials and techniques employed by Shakespeare's contemporaries. Not only was it to be a theatre that looked Elizabethan, but the actors were to employ original practices, the audience would stand in a pit below the stage instead of in rows of seats, the musicians would use Elizabethan instruments (originally the

183

plays were accompanied by a small band or orchestra providing incidental music) and the actors would wear authentic costumes made in traditional materials, colours and design.

The original Globe was built in 1598, and was destroyed by fire in 1613. It was replaced by another theatre of the same name in 1614. This was closed by the Puritans in 1642, during the English Civil War. Not content with just closing it, they actually pulled it down two years later, simply to make sure nobody could use it. Perhaps some actors had been creeping back into the building at night to perform.

In Shakespeare's time, the theatre was round and built of wood with a thatched partial roof, with a raised stage against a back wall, a musicians' gallery above the stage, the pit for the audience taking up most of the rest of the 'Wooden O'. Behind the pit, on three sides of the circle, were a few rows of seats, on galleries, for the aristocracy and the rich. The stage and the seats were covered by a thatched roof and the pit was open to the elements. It was rare for a performance to be cancelled because of inclement weather: too much money would be lost and most companies of actors shared the profits.

Almost from the moment he arrived, rebuilding the Globe became Sam Wanamaker's dream and obsession, but all dreams get put on the back burner when you have a wife and children and need to make a living. Sam chose to make that living in England. He made his acting debut in London in 1952, and then, in 1957, became director of the New Shakespeare Theatre in Liverpool.

He was a member of the Royal Shakespeare Company in Stratford from 1959 and I remember him as one of the greatest Iagos I ever saw when he played the role to Paul Robeson's towering Othello that season. Sam was a gifted film actor and director, appearing in many and varied movie roles and on television, but his great love was acting and directing Shakespeare plays, which he continued to do for the rest of his life. He was a busy star actor who could easily have settled for that and had a varied and happy life, but there always burned in his head the dream of Shakespeare's theatre on the banks of the Thames.

So he started – raising money, making speeches, bullying, cajoling, begging. And it took an American with a great love of English theatre, and specially Shakespeare, to wade through the various layers of bureaucracy and inertia to break ground on Shakespeare's Globe Theatre, built as close as humanly possible to the site of the original Globe, on Bankside, on the south bank of the Thames.

Authenticity was the watchword. The new Globe is the first public building in London since the Great Fire of London, in 1666, to be allowed a thatched roof. The London Fire Service said it was a fire hazard; Wanamaker insisted on real thatch for the reconstruction. It was a stand-off until modern technology and fireproofing came to the rescue and the permit was granted. And this was only one of a million similar hurdles that had to be leaped to build the Globe, which is, no contest, the best and most beautiful theatre built in my lifetime.

It opened on 27 May 1997, but, tragically, Sam wasn't there to see it. He had died in 1993, four years before the vision that he fought for so long to realise was actually completed. He did, however, know that the theatre was in the process of being built, that it would happen, that it would be his memorial, and that generations to come would have the extraordinary experience, whether they attended a play or even if they took a river cruise along the Thames, of seeing a Shakespearean theatre of the type the playwright himself would recognise, standing in the area that had been Shakespeare's and Marlowe's equivalent of the West End, over four hundred years earlier.

Shakespeare's Globe is today one of the great success stories of the contemporary theatre. On any night, whatever the weather, you can see droves of young people from all over the world stuffed into the pit enjoying the play. Mark Rylance, the first artistic director, developed a performance ethos directly in line with Sam Wanamaker's dream: of all-male casts (there were no women acting on stage when the plays were first performed), original practices and music, research into Elizabethan movement and speech, wonderful programmes for children, new plays based on period sources, even all-women companies (this was *not* a Shakespearean practice) with great actors given the opportunity to perform cross-gender – Vanessa Redgrave as Prospero, Janet McTeer as Petruchio, Mark Rylance himself as Cleopatra. There is a vital and unmissable mix of the ancient and modern and, far from being merely a museum celebrating a long-dead playwright, Shakespeare's Globe is alive and looking confidently towards the future, as very few other theatres can.

This is exactly what Sam Wanamaker wanted to build for us. And more. Thank you, Sam.

DAME JUDI DENCH: SMOKE GETS IN YOUR EYES

ALDWYCH THEATRE, 1998

Dame Judi Dench, says Richard Eyre, can do anything, and does. Hers is one of the few names – Maggie Smith, Diana Rigg and Vanessa Redgrave are the other actresses in that exclusive club – that can start a queue at the box office just by being above a West End marquee.

When Eyre directed her in David Hare's play, *Amy's View*, the impact was felt all over the theatrical world, on Broadway as well as at the National Theatre and the West End. In it she played Esmé, an ageing actress, and life followed art in more ways than one, although Hare insists he didn't know it at the time he was writing.

In the play, Esmé guesses that her offstage daughter is pregnant. While *Amy's View* was in rehearsal at the National, Judi's daughter, Finty, gave birth to her grandson, Sam. What made the incident in the play especially poignant is that Judi and her husband Michael Williams had both failed to guess that Finty was pregnant, and the first they knew of the event was when Sam was born, two months prematurely.

When Judi was on Broadway, it seemed for a horrible few days as though there would be another case of life imitating art. In the script, Esmé loses her husband, Bernard. Back in London, Michael Williams fell dangerous ill with pleurisy, and Judi took time off from the play to return to England and nurse him. He survived that episode but was to die far too young, in 2001, from cancer.

Amy's View received excellent reviews: the *Guardian* confirmed that 'Dench is excellent at giving portraits of actresses'; the *Times* said, 'A major dramatist has written a strong, rich play, and a major actress has done him proud'; the *New Yorker* thought that 'Broadway doesn't beckon – it positively waves and shouts.' Judi was worried that the part might go to Meryl Streep or Glenn Close – both of whom came to London to see the play – but her fears were, fortunately, groundless.

Amy's View did indeed go to Broadway, where it played to full houses every night. The reception on the other side of the Atlantic was to prove equally enthusiastic, with *Variety* summing it up as 'quite simply bliss', and the *New York Times* saying, 'Those who have seen Ms Dench only in movies will discover qualities that a camera can't capture: a force of will-power, concentration, technique and sheer radiance that brands her presence in our memories.'

One story from the London run of the play, at the Aldwych Theatre, epitomises the placidity of Judi Dench's temperament and the reason why everybody who has ever worked with her adores her. Esmé in *Amy's View* smokes throughout the play, and on one night, during its run at the Aldwych, a man sitting in the front row of the stalls made a great fuss about the smoke that inevitably drifted towards him, coughing loudly and fanning the smoke away with his hands, which flailed about, distractingly.

Dame Judi couldn't help but notice but carried on regardless. In the interval she summoned the theatre manager to her dressing room, and asked him to identify the man who had made the fuss. The man had, in fact, already complained to the ushers, who were deeply embarrassed at the commotion, and the manager already knew where the man was sitting.

As the interval drew to a close and the audience returned to their seats, the manager approached the man and gave him a small package. The man looked surprised. 'This is from Dame Judi,' the manager explained. Embarrassed but intrigued, the man opened the package to find a small tin. Inside were two cough sweets and a note that simply read, 'From one non-smoker to another.' There was no waving about of hands for the rest of the play, just a quietly well-behaved man with a smile on his face.

WHO NEEDS VIAGRA?

DONMAR WAREHOUSE, LONDON, 1998

If Helen's was the face that launched a thousand ships, then Nicole Kidman's was the body that fulfilled several thousand heterosexual male fantasies, stripping off in public (albeit in dimmed lighting) in a West End theatre where the seats were gratifyingly close to the stage, and a great view was had by nearly all. She was also responsible for launching a phrase, by one of my colleagues, Charles Spencer, that has entered the national vocabulary.

The play was *The Blue Room*, based on Arthur Schnitzler's *La Ronde* and 'freely adapted' by David Hare. Sam Mendes was the director, long before he won an Oscar for *American Beauty*. Then, he was the theatrical *wunderkind* who had turned the Donmar Warehouse into the trendiest theatre in town. He was artistic director of the 250-seat Covent Garden playhouse, which was named after Donald Albery and Margot Fonteyn because it was their money that had enabled the old fruit warehouse to be turned into a theatre in the first place, and he had the knack of generating excitement with every play or musical he chose.

The Blue Room opened on 22 September 1998 starring Nicole Kidman and Iain Glen, each playing numerous roles. The play was a series of short scenes, each a sexual coupling, with one of the couple then going on to another sexual encounter with a new partner.

It was the combination of the Donmar's reputation, David Hare's background as a leading playwright and Sam Mendes's unbroken record as the hottest director in town that tempted Nicole Kidman, then still married to Tom Cruise and part of Hollywood royalty, onto the London stage. *La Ronde* is a classic that has been adapted in dozens of versions, and every film star wants to be seen in a major play.

What finally mattered was, depending on your point of view, nothing to do with the play or the performers – and your point of view may have depended on where you were seated. Because what most people remember about that production is that they got to see Miss Kidman naked. Even though she was discreetly draped or actually clothed for most of the performance, and they saw a lot more of Iain Glen's nude body, even turning cartwheels, than of hers, it was Miss Kidman, naked, that stayed in everyone's mind.

We critics all sat there pretending not to notice that Mrs Tom Cruise had no clothes on. We were professionals, this was our job, you can't impress us and, heaven forfend, we *never* leer. But we noticed. Oh, yes, those of us not yet dead noticed. As she shared one bed after another with Mr Glen, the audience was simultaneously peering at *Mr* Tom Cruise to see how he was reacting. So, as Princess Diana might have put it, the stage was at times a little crowded, as there were in effect three people in a play written for two.

The Blue Room was a palpable hit, every performance was sold out, and Miss Kidman's, ahem, acting abilities were sung to the skies. In fact, she's a fine stage actress, a quality totally erased in the audience's consciousness by her fleeting moment of nudity. And Charlie Spencer's phrase, which you've surely heard many times in various contexts by now, was that seeing Nicole Kidman, undressed on stage, was 'pure theatrical Viagra'.

MISS JONES DOES CLEOPATRA

BARBICAN THEATRE, 2000

'Ooh! Miss Jones!' The catchphrase of Leonard Rossiter, playing Rigsby, the seedy landlord with pretensions to an artistic nature he wouldn't recognise if it slapped him in the face, was one of the regular features of the 1970s television sitcom *Rising Damp*, and the (attempted) relationship between Rigsby and his female tenant, Miss Jones, played with a gawky charm by Frances de la Tour, was one of the most popular aspects of the show.

Saddled with that role, as she invariably will be for the rest of her life, de la Tour has had to endure comparisons to Miss Jones in reviews for the wide variety of roles she has, subsequently, played on stage. And these have been many.

Many will not have been surprised to see her disguised as a nun in *The Pope and the Witch*, a madcap comic romp at the Comedy Theatre in 1992. They would also have been astonished to see her in Edward Albee's *Three Tall Women* at Wyndham's three years later in 1995, where, a million miles from her public image, she played a cool, classy and elegant middle-aged woman.

So, to theatregoers if not television viewers, it came as no great surprise – though it was clearly going to be a challenge – to hear that she was cast, by the RSC, as Cleopatra. It was a role she had first played at Stratford and afterwards, at the RSC's then London home (and why ever did they leave?), the Barbican.

Her Antony was Alan Bates, who gave a characteristically

strong and still (despite his years) sexy performance: we could understand why this ageing soldier inspired so much passion in the Serpent of Old Nile, and she in a Roman general enchanted by the exoticism of the East. Bates was to die, of cancer, three years later, robbing us of one of our best actors, who had been at the forefront of British theatre from the moment he appeared, as Cliff, in John Osborne's *Look Back in Anger* at the Royal Court in 1956 (see 'Kenneth Tynan and *Look Back in Anger*').

Bates died too young at 69 – he had been recently knighted, had won a Tony on Broadway for his role in *Fortune's Fool*, and seemed likely to have many more years of older parts in the classics still ahead of him, on Broadway as well as in the West End.

His Cleopatra, Frances de la Tour, is an actress who has always been brave, always taken artistic risks, and she now decided on the biggest gamble of her career. The major change to her performance between Warwickshire and the City was that the flash of naked flesh under her robe, when she applied the asp to her breast in the most famous suicide scene in all theatre, if not all history, would now be more than that: by the time she reached the City she had decided to play the scene completely naked.

Actors often talk about baring themselves on stage emotionally but to remove your clothes completely, unless you happen to be gorgeous (and even then it takes some nerve), is another matter entirely. For a woman in her mid-fifties, with a figure that advertisers would describe as 'normal' rather than lithe or even statuesque, it took real courage.

But, artistically, it made sense. What more telling way to show the complete vulnerability of a woman who had once been shielded and covered by 'the divinity that doth hedge a king'? The fact that de la Tour, with the greatest respect, isn't a great beauty (though, as *Three Tall Women* proved, she is more of a looker than given credit for), made this vulnerability all the more moving. There was nothing lurid, or smutty, or exploitative about it, and for once the time-honoured phrase (which of course has nothing to do with honour, and everything to do with ticket sales), that 'it's really necessary for the play' actually meant something.

The *coup de grâce* came with the fact that, having died in front of our eyes on stage, because there was no curtain to come down or scenery change to hide behind, Miss de la Tour simply got up and walked off stage, and in those few moments added, as if it were possible, to the dignity and pathos of the occasion. She was walking into the wings: Cleopatra was disappearing from the warmth of life into the deep freeze of History.

A gutsy lady indeed.

DAWN FRENCH'S BOTTOM

ALBERY THEATRE, 2001

There were no actresses in any of Shakespeare's plays, which is why there are so many wonderful parts for men and so few for women. Yes, Lady Macbeth, of course, Cleopatra, and Juliet, but none has the width and breadth of Hamlet, Macbeth, Brutus, Henry V and the rest. Cross-dressing was, therefore, *de rigueur* in Shakespeare's time and becoming increasing so in our own. Mark Rylance made a memorable Cleopatra at the Globe a few seasons ago, and Janet McTeer was a more than usually swaggering Petruchio in an all-woman *Taming of the Shrew* in the same theatre.

But, until comedienne Dawn French played Bottom in Matthew Francis's West End production of *A Midsummer Night's Dream* at the Albery Theatre in March 2001, I had never thought of the old donkey as a travesty role. Nor, I must admit, had I ever thought of the various meanings of the character's name until Miss French waved her ample posterior at me from the stage of the Duke of York's Theatre.

I have seen many bottoms of all kinds in my time at the theatre, but the sight of the good-natured Dawn French jitterbugging to Benny Goodman, her face beaming with goodwill as she relishes the chance for her Bottom to get involved in play-acting, is one of the most memorable.

The director set the play in the early 1940s, during the war, with the 'rude mechanicals' being a group of ladies from the local Women's Institute, led by Miss French. A bit gimmicky, you might think, but almost as soon as it began it banished

195

more conventional productions in its genial midsummer warmth, stirring as many memories of the magical *Wind in the Willows* – with its long languid Edwardian afternoons in the depths of the countryside – as it did of Shakespeare or the Spitfire-filled skies of the 1940s that Francis has chosen as his backdrop.

French, as Bottom, was able to project the comic persona for which her fans had come to see her, while also definitely playing a part – a difficult feat, but one that she pulled off. This could have been a gimmick, what producer Katherine Doré called '*Vicar of Dibley* Shakespeare', but it was an artistic success. Interesting then that Doré is one of the few women producers around (Sonia Friedman being another major player), and that one of her main claims to fame was producing an all-male (well, all-male-swans, anyway) *Swan Lake* – Matthew Bourne's version of the Russian classic. So it is not surprising either that she should cast against usual sexual stereotype, or that the casting should work so well.

And so does the rest of the production, from a beautiful human (Jemma Redgrave) playing Titania, the fairy queen, to a remarkably beautiful forest – designed by Bourne's *Swan Lake* designer Lez Brotherston – for the lovers to get lost in, and for Puck to work his magic in: a happy change from the all-too-frequent couple of tyres on a pole.

Dawn's astonishment at the transformation scene is one of the many amusing extras of a woman playing Bottom: her creature gets not just the ears of an ass but also the appendage between her legs of something frequently thought of admiringly in terms of a donkey, and this gives her ample (but not gratuitous) comic mileage.

Which is why the impression that remains, now some years since the production opened, is that of Miss French suggesting that the WI's real talent is not for jam so much as ham. It also confirmed Dawn French as a stage actress, and, though she's superb on television, could the theatre please have her back again, even if only for just one more stage comedy?

MADONNA DEFINITELY NOT UP
FOR GRABS

WYNDHAM'S THEATRE, 2002

Wembley in the West End? Or when is a play a pop concert? When the pop singer Madonna is involved, of course. Like so many Hollywood stars (of uneven provenance) she wanted her moment of glory in the West End. And what Madonna wants, Madonna gets. She chose her vehicle carefully and finally settled on *Up For Grabs*, an Australian drama by the respected playwright, David Williamson, directed by Laurence Boswell. Unfortunately, someone thought it would be a great idea to reset it from Sydney to New York. It doesn't seem to have occurred to that someone, or indeed anyone, that changing the location meant changing the nature of the play.

The play, as written, is about the venality and greed of art dealers in Australia, where the art market is separated by the Pacific Ocean from the dominant markets of London and New York. Placing it in the centre of the world art market rendered the plot absurd and the premise preposterous. Sydney is not New York and the shenanigans that might succeed in Oz simply would be laughed out of any NY gallery.

Madonna played a ruthless art dealer who is out to make a fortune from a Jackson Pollock painting, and is prepared to lie and cheat and sell her marriage for it – and she nearly succeeds. This might work in Sydney but the NY sharpies she comes up against would have sniffed her out in a heartbeat.

It was not Madonna's first theatrical experience. In 1988, she had played a small but crucial role in David Mamet's *Speed the Plow.* I saw that performance and it did her some credit. She came across as possessing considerable poise and a modicum of humour, everything that Mamet had written in, and a bit more. But here, in *Up For Grabs*, she was carrying the entire play, and it was too heavy for her.

Madonna bashed on, regardless. From all accounts, despite the near-hysteria from the tabloid press, the paparazzi following her to and from rehearsals, and the heightened security, she behaved well. Insiders agreed that her demeanour in rehearsals was exemplary. She worked very hard, and the other actors admired her persistence and perfectionism. She didn't 'pull a star', insist on special treatment, turn up late or leave early.

Up For Grabs opened at Wyndham's Theatre on 23 May 2002. The audience on opening night was more showbizzy (and specifically pop) than usual, with the likes of Jonny Lee Miller, Stella McCartney, Donatella Versace and Sting stuffing the stalls. Madonna got a richly undeserved (except for effort) standing ovation. The critics didn't much care for it but that wasn't a problem, since the ten-week run was sold out almost the moment booking opened. Her audiences loved her. For them she could do no wrong and she certainly has the sort of star presence that made a sell-out run understandable, even though she refused to play matinées. Whether that was due to fatigue or recording commitments remains unclear.

But, however professional she may have been on stage, she could not quite shake the habits of a pop superstar and the story became not the play but the security arrangements. Her 'advisers' had the stage raised by one and a half feet so that overenthusiastic fans would find it hard to climb onto it to touch their heroine. As far as I know, nobody ever tried, but this played havoc with the sight lines (which is not a problem at a rock concert where the fans stand up anyway and nobody can see anything).

What was funnier was to see the sumo-wrestler-style bouncers parading in the aisles during a West End drama, earpieces in place, curly cables down their nonexistent necks, muttering darkly into invisible microphones throughout the play. On opening night, to add to the chaos, all the pop stars and fashionistas brought their own stern-looking security guards, thus causing a traffic jam on the side aisles. When the play got boring, or when the actors were difficult to see because of the raised stage, the entertainment was clearly in the aisles as enormous men bumped into each other, each trying to protect a different star. Still more giants glowered at the side of the stage in case anyone was foolish enough to think of leaving their seat and racing to the footlights. In my case, although I was longing to race to the exit, I didn't dare, in case they had a shoot-to-kill policy.

Given the hysteria Madonna generates on any public appearance, it was probably foolhardy to expect her to behave like an actress in a West End play, rather than a superstar pretending to act. But it was all new to us in theatreland and required a certain extra suspension of disbelief to imagine that the well-dressed woman on stage was a character in a play, no matter how hard she tried. She was Madonna.

THE LONGEST-RUNNING SHOW IN THE WORLD

ST MARTIN'S THEATRE, 2002

It was, if not a glittering occasion, then certainly a glamorous one. For once, the paparazzi who habitually cluster around the entrance to the Ivy had their backs to this, London's most fashionable theatre restaurant, and their faces, hidden behind the tools of their trade, pointed across the road at the St Martin's Theatre.

They were, however, unable to push and jostle for the best photo, since they were kept at a decent (if not respectful) distance by a line of police, along with the usual gaggle of die-hard royalty watchers.

They were all there to witness the arrival of the Queen and the Duke of Edinburgh at the theatre for the fiftieth-anniversary performance of Agatha Christie's *The Mousetrap*.

Fifty years is, of course, an extraordinary length for a show to run, and the production, which began its London life at the neighbouring Ambassadors Theatre, opening there on 25 November 1952, has been at the St Martin's since 1974.

The first major record that *The Mousetrap* took was 'longest ever run in a London theatre', which it achieved in April 1958, when it broke the record previously held by World War One hit *Chu Chin Chow*. Since then we have had massively long runs by the likes of the musicals *Cats*, *Les Misérables* and *Miss Saigon* – and of straight plays such as *The Woman in Black*. But nothing is likely ever to match *The Mousetrap*.

As the Queen arrived at the theatre she will have been well

aware that the origins of the play lay with the celebration of her grandmother's (Queen Mary's) eightieth birthday. Queen Mary (or 'Gan Gan' as she was referred to by the Queen in the ground-breaking 1969 documentary *Royal Family*) was, despite being famously reserved and regal, a much-loved figure by the time of her eightieth birthday in 1947.

This occasion had been marked by the commissioning, by the BBC, of an Agatha Christie radio play originally called *Three Blind Mice*. However, when the broadcast of a shortened version of the story proved a great success, Christie, who was a very astute playwright as well as the multimillionaire queen of detective fiction, decided she would turn it into a play, which she decided to call (for copyright reasons), *The Mousetrap*. The name was taken from *Hamlet*, where an unpleasant truth is revealed, in the play within the play.

The Mousetrap opened at the Ambassadors Theatre in the year that Elizabeth II came to the throne, so it was a very happy coincidence that the Queen's visit to this gala performance on 25 November 2002 should come as part of the year-long celebrations of her own fiftieth anniversary as Queen.

The Queen is known to have a fondness for the 1950s and for tradition in general – indeed, it's an essential part of her job. Not for nothing was she a great fan of *Dad's Army* during its 1960s and early 1970s heyday.

Going to see *The Mousetrap*, as she was reminded by her 2002 visit, is very much like taking a trip in a time machine. The St Martin's Theatre is a very attractively panelled auditorium that looks more like an English country house than a West End theatre, and the play's setting, construction, plot and characters are all very 1950s.

The setting – a snowbound hotel – relies on the fact that, long before the advent of mobile phones, the telephone line has been cut off, ostensibly by a storm. There is a mildly hysterical gay character who in many ways represents the seriously held view of the time that all gays were slightly wrong in the head, of overly excitable dispositions and, by implication, could be 'cured' by the right woman, plenty of fresh air and some hearty soup.

The play went well, the Queen beamed, plenty of refreshment was served – the royals like a drink, though the two greatest imbibers, the Queen Mother and Princess Margaret, are no longer with us – and, at the end of the performance, at the curtain call, the traditional appeal to the audience by a cast member was made – 'Please tell no one the secret of *The Mousetrap*, but instead keep it locked in your hearts' – with a particular look at that point at the royal party!

The cast were presented to the Queen, as were two of the original members, Lord (Richard) Attenborough and his wife, Sheila Sim. Lord Attenborough said, '*The Mousetrap* is like a London institution – like the ravens in the Tower of London' (which is overstating it a bit), while Dame Agatha's great-great-grandchildren, Joshua and Max Clementson, presented the Queen with a posy and a model of a mousetrap.

The Queen promised not to divulge the play's secret – which is an astonishingly well-kept one, and returned to Buckingham Palace looking as if she, like millions before her, had thoroughly enjoyed the evening.

What is the secret, not of the play, but of its success? Agatha Christie herself said of it, 'It's not really frightening. It's not really horrible. It's not really a farce. But it has a little of all these things and perhaps that satisfies a lot of people.' All these things are true, though there is a real shock with a murder – and a scream on stage always provides a frisson.

Were the play to be staged now, in the style that it is, it would be unlikely to run more than a few weeks in the West End (though it could certainly have a touring life). But that's not the reason that tourists and curious Brits still flock to it. It's precisely because it is so old-fashioned and the amazing fact of its longevity that attracts; but the pleasant surprise it that, given all this, it remains, like all Christie's work, wonderfully well crafted.

It will undoubtedly and deservedly continue well into this new century (and probably the next), and if, as seems likely, Queen Elizabeth II celebrates (like Queen Victoria) not just her Golden Jubilee as Queen but her Diamond, then it's quite possible that she will pay another gala visit to the St Martin's, taking Princes William and Harry along to introduce, as members of the public have done, a new generation of their family to one of London's strange but enjoyable theatrical traditions.

JUDY CAMPBELL AT JERMYN STREET

JERMYN STREET THEATRE, 2003

I first directed the amazing Judy Campbell in the *Jermyn Street Revue* at its eponymous Theatre in 2003. My wife, Ruth Leon, directed Judy, with Stefan Bednarczyk on the piano, in her one-woman (plus Stefan, of course) show, *Where Are the Songs We Sung?*, at the King's Head, Islington, and this was a show she was to reprise, whenever she was asked, for the pleasure it gave her and her many admirers to see her back on stage.

When I once asked her whether she was not getting rather tired of this sort of thing (she was pushing ninety, after all), she said, 'No, because you see, I live alone in Chelsea now, and when I'm on stage there's always some nice old boy who wants to take me out to dinner afterwards, so it saves on the cooking and washing up, as well as giving me something to do after the show!'

She was, naturally, being modest, because she still had the stage presence, the sense of mischief, the timing and, in a way, the beauty that had captivated Londoners during the Blitz and made Noël Coward determined to work with her.

She had come to his attention when performing in the 1940 revue *New Faces*, at the Comedy Theatre. The Dorothy Parker monologue she was supposed to recite had been mislaid at the last minute, so the composer Eric Maschwitz gave her a song to sing. He wrote it overnight, the week before the revue opened, just as a stopgap until the monologue was found, and over Judy's protests that she was an actress and sometime comedienne, not a singer. The show needed a song in that spot, he told her, and here was the song; learn it, sing it, and shut up.

She decided that the only way to make it work was to act it out, to make a little drama of it so the audience would be given a small play rather than just a song. It helped that she looked stunning, her tall slim figure, her chiselled beauty and mass of dark hair set off perfectly by a white evening dress and her mother's feather boa. The result was sensational, the show ran for a year and a star was born.

Coward, after seeing it, took her to dinner at the Savoy Grill and made her repeat her performance for the benefit of their fellow diners. He told her, 'It takes talent to put over a song when you haven't got a voice. One day we'll act together.'

Indeed they did, with a wartime tour of *Present Laughter* (in which she created the role of Joanna), *This Happy Breed* (in which she created the part of Ethel) and *Blithe Spirit* (in which she played Elvira).

It was one of her many charms that she could recreate this tour in our minds, even those of us who were too young to remember it, as she sat on the little stage of a pub theatre in Islington in the new millennium, transporting us back to the dark but strangely heady days when our resistance really was toughened with every Blitz, as Coward wrote in the song 'London Pride'.

During the tour, she told us, in that crisp, clear, upper-class voice of the last theatrical century, when they were playing a remote theatre in the North of England in the middle of a freezing winter, she and Noël went on-stage, their teeth chattering. Noël wore his trademark dinner jacket (where an overcoat would have been more seasonal); she wore the inevitable white evening dress that showed off her figure to full advantage (although she would have preferred longjohns and several layers of woollies).

As they acted together on a sofa, in a touchingly tender scene, he put rather more passion than usual into his performance, reaching out with both hands (which he slid beneath the satin) cupping her breasts and remaining there for the several minutes of the scene, creating an electrically charged sexual tension in the audience.

'At last!' she told a breathless Jermyn Street audience. 'At last, I thought, I've done it! I've managed to excite Noël Coward, make him want a woman! Only to have him come up to me after the curtain fell and say, "Thank you for that, darling. That was the first time my hands have been warm for weeks!"'

Judy aged remarkably gracefully. She would tell you her age at the drop of a hat, knowing how, at every stage up to the very last, she looked decades younger. She was old enough to remember when, growing up in Grantham, where her father ran a theatre and cinema, one of their most regular customers was little Margaret Roberts, the grocer's daughter – who went on to become Margaret Thatcher, prime minister of the United Kingdom from 1979 to 1990.

Judy married David Birkin, a suitably dashing naval officer. For more than twenty years, she worked only when she judged that the family needed the money. David was terribly wounded in the war and she gave up the theatre to look after him and their three children – Andrew (who became a great expert on *Peter Pan* and wrote *The Lost Boys*), Linda (who, with her husband, has looked after the royal palaces for the Queen), and Jane Birkin, who was to achieve her own brand of fame as the other half of the partnership that engendered one of the great hits of the Sixties, 'Je t'Aime, Moi Non Plus', with Serge Gainsbourg.

Jane has lived in Paris for almost her entire adult life, although remaining close to her beloved mother. Judy used to tell the story of the occasion when she was heading to Paris to visit Jane but knew that, when she arrived, Jane would be out filming and the weather forecast was terrible. 'Don't worry, Mum,' said Jane, 'I don't have a key to get into my flat, just an electronic keypad. All you have to do is to tap in the year of my birth which, being my mother, you remember, and, *voilà*, the door will open.' Simple, right?

Judy duly arrived, with her luggage, keyed in the date – and heard no reassuring little click. She pushed. The door remained firmly closed. She tried again. Then again. Eventually, after hours of waiting, Ms Birkin returned to find her tired and frustrated mother waiting on the pavement in the pouring rain, wet, exhausted and, for Judy, quite cross. She explained that she had typed in the birth date as instructed but—

Jane cut into her story. 'Oh, my God! I forgot to tell you! I lied to the doorknob about my age!'

It was this sort of story, beautifully told, along with an ability to sing and do a gentle, Edwardian dance, while well into her eighties, that made Judy such good company on stage and off, and that one-woman (plus Stefan) run, with her brushing back the years, and reprising her greatest hit, will live in my memory and in the memory of everybody who knew her and all those who saw her on stage. The show was called *Where Are The Songs We Sung?*, the title of one of Noël's most nostalgic songs, but the song darling Judy sang was, of course, the one Eric Maschwitz wrote for her all those years ago and *pace* Vera Lynn, the song nobody could put over as well, even or perhaps especially after she stopped singing it and simply stood there and inhabited it. Judy Campbell, who died in June 2004 aged 88, will always be with me whenever anyone sings 'A Nightingale Sang in Berkeley Square'.

CURTAIN CALL TAKES A BOW

PLAYHOUSE THEATRE, 2004

Some curtain calls are great fun, some are noisy, some self-congratulatory, some modest. What they all do is to offer actors and audience alike an opportunity for a release of emotion at the end of a well-performed show, be it comedy, drama or musical.

Musicals tend to generate more energy, so they tend to beg for and get a more high-octane reception. Often they are an indispensable part of the show, with a specially choreographed song and dance as the cast are taking their bows, sometimes they reprise the best songs from the show, as a sort of generalised encore. Straight plays tend to line up the cast, allow the audience to see them smile their own smiles, and the whole event is over in seconds. Even the liveliest farce doesn't usually generate a curtain call of any note, even when the actors stay in character.

What is unique, in my experience, is the case of a moving drama, when the curtain call generated as much emotion as any of the preceding scenes, and in some ways created the *coup de théâtre* that was the most memorable part of the production.

The play was David Grindley's production of R C Sherriff's *Journey's End*, a sensibly old-fashioned staging of this 1929 play about the horrors of World War One. There was, quite rightly, no attempt to update it. This is a play not about war in general, but specifically about the extraordinary carnage, most of it pointless, generated on the Western Front. The production caught something of the mood of the time, and the tragic waste of young life was heartbreakingly evident.

The play is set in the dugout of a British front-line trench in the spring of 1918, with the expected German assault – the Kaiser's final push – about to happen. By the end, all the characters are dead, killed in the attack, and by then we in the audience have had time to get to know them and mourn the uselessness of their passing.

At the end of the play (don't read this if you haven't yet seen it), all the officers having been killed in the German attack, the curtain falls as dust and rubble fall into their dugout, the destruction by German artillery continues, and the audience are nearly deafened by the sound of shells dropping and machine guns clattering.

This noise – which gives an uncomfortably realistic idea of the noise made by, and fear generated during, an attack – carries on in the dark, and then, after a very brief silence, there is the sound of the last post as the curtain rises. The cast, taking their curtain call, are lined up in front of a massive war memorial wall with a seemingly endless roll call of the names of the dead.

Staying not just in character but standing to attention and unsmiling, the cast take their applause as if they were ghosts, statues on a war memorial. The effect is incredibly moving, the lists of names, mirroring the war-memorial crosses that record an entire generation of young men and that stand in every village, however small, in the countryside of Britain, France and Flanders.

This production started its West End life at the Comedy Theatre, before moving to the Playhouse, and then to the Duke of York's, and in the course of its long run had several casts, all excellent. Terence Rattigan, another playwright with an uncanny ability to engender tears, in one of his best plays, *The Browning Version* (itself a real tear jerker at the end), has his lead character observe, 'Sometimes an anticlimax can be surprisingly effective.'

This production of *Journey's End*, Sherriff's sole masterpiece, concluded not with an anticlimax but silence, a post-curtain pageant whose simplicity, immobility and silence allowed the audience to applaud the actors while unashamedly letting the tears that had moistened their eyes during the play now course down their cheeks at this most surprising and effective of curtain calls.

REMEMBERING ROBERT
BADDELEY

DRURY LANE, 2005

The saloon at Drury Lane was full of guests enjoying
themselves. Outside, it was cold and dark, inside warm, well lit
and inviting.

Perhaps the strangest, and certainly the tastiest, tradition in
British theatre was about to take place – and, appropriately
enough for Britain's most historic playhouse, it was a home-
grown one. Or home-baked, you might say.

A round of applause from the cast of the Lane's latest hit
musical, Mel Brooks's *The Producers*, greeted the arrival of an
extraordinary cake, decorated to look like a scene from the
show.

A hush was eventually established, even from the few
thespians still too preoccupied with themselves and conver-
sations about their careers (an occupational hazard in the
theatre) to be paying much attention to tradition, and then the
Ceremony of the Baddeley Cake began.

There was a speech about Robert Baddeley, a few words
about the modern-day pastry cooks who made that night's
cake, a few quips from members of the cast – including Conleth
Hill (playing camp director Roger Debris) – and then the
assembled actors and guests raised their glasses to Robert
Baddeley's memory. *Robert who?*

Robert Baddeley was a pastry chef, born in 1733, who
worked for a while for an actor and theatre manager, Samuel
Foote. Catching the acting bug off his employer, he joined

211

David Garrick's theatre company at Drury Lane in 1760, the year that King George III came to the throne.

Baddeley, having made his choice, was at least consistent – he stayed with the company for the rest of his life, dying in harness, during the run of Sheridan's *The School For Scandal*. He created the role of Moses in the play's original production and was getting ready to go on stage to play the part on 19 November 1794, when he was seized with a fit, and taken home, where he died the next evening.

During his time at the Lane (as the theatre is known within the profession) he specialised in comic parts – especially as old men or foreigners (and preferably both). He played the classic role of an old Danish courtier (Polonius in *Hamlet*) and was also considered a good Bottom in Shakespeare's *A Midsummer Night's Dream*.

Baddeley loved the companionship that being part of a resident company offered, so his will stipulated that:

> I hereby direct that the sum of one hundred pounds stock in the three per cent consolidated bank annuities may be purchased directly after my decease . . . to produce as nearly as possible the sum of three hundred pounds which . . . I direct to be applied and expended in the purchase of a Twelfth Night cake or cakes and wine and punch or both of them which . . . it is my request that the ladies and gentlemen performers of Drury Lane Theatre will do me the favour to accept on Twelfth Night in every year in the Green Room . . .

The celebration of Twelfth Night is a ritual that has faded in importance over the years, but at Drury Lane Mr Baddeley's bequest has ensured that it remains a highlight of the theatrical year, with a large cake, decorated in a way to reflect the show then running, being enjoyed by all those present.

Originally, the evening was organised by the directors of the theatre, but since 1822 this has been the responsibility of the Drury Lane Theatrical Fund. This Fund was set up in 1776, the year of the American Revolution, by no less a figure than

David Garrick himself, and has the distinction of being the oldest theatrical charity in existence. In fact, Baddeley had been one of the Fund's trustees.

The first cake was cut in 1796 and the ceremony has taken place every year since, apart from a baker's dozen (appropriately) of occasions when the theatre has been 'dark' – i.e. no shows were playing there – or war has made it impossible.

The punch bowl, where the delicious (and secret) recipe for punch produces its annual appearance, was provided by the company of *My Fair Lady* in 1963, celebrating 300 years of the Drury Lane company's existence. The cast of *Miss Saigon* have the distinction of having ploughed through more Baddeley cakes (ten) than any other at Drury Lane.

Strangely enough, Robert Baddeley's ghost has not been sighted at the frequently haunted theatre, but that's probably because ghosts tend to be fundamentally unhappy, whereas Mr Baddeley's memory – and spirit – is cheerfully toasted every year and he must surely have no cause for complaint, or haunting, given that his love of the theatre and sense of belonging is still very much a part of the continuing life of Drury Lane.

GRACE KELLY'S GHOST AT THE OLD VIC

OLD VIC, MAY 2005

The Philadelphia Story by Philip Barry was, in fact, owned by its star and leading lady, Katharine Hepburn. When Hollywood branded her 'box-office poison' in 1938, she asked Barry to write a play that she could take on tour and onto Broadway. It was a huge success, thus proving that Hepburn had been right when she claimed that Hollywood was casting her in the wrong scripts, thus shooting themselves in the foot, and that they, not she, were responsible for turning her into 'box-office poison'.

The studios had to eat crow when, in 1940, she returned in triumph to Hollywood where she sold the film rights to *The Philadelphia Story* to Louis B Mayer for a reported £250,000. She also insisted on a veto of producer, director and adaptor. Cary Grant and James Stewart were her hand-picked co-stars, George Cukor was her director and Donald Ogden Stewart adapted Barry's script into a screenplay.

Her terms, unheard of then or since, were that, although she would take no salary, she wanted (and got) a fabulous 45 per cent of the profits. She didn't win the Oscar that year but both Stewarts did – Jimmy and her adaptor, Donald Ogden – and her movie was nominated for six of the gold statuettes, including that for Best Picture. Kate was back on top of the Hollywood heap, which she had left, stinking, a scant two years earlier.

Not content with a play and a movie, Kate's play was to have another incarnation. In 1956, Cole Porter wrote one of his last and best classic scores for a musical adaptation of *The Philadelphia Story*. Now called *High Society* but retaining its plot, its storyline, its characters and all its charm, it now starred Bing Crosby, Frank Sinatra, Celeste Holm and the uniquely wonderful Louis Armstrong. In the all-important role of Tracy Lord, Hepburn's own favourite part, was the Ice Maiden herself, the non-singing Grace Kelly.

Her glacial blonde beauty and perfectly chiselled features were ideal for the part of a rich Philadelphia princess, which, in fact, she was, although Grace's family had *earned* their fortune, while Tracy's had inherited theirs. And indeed the film landed her her greatest starring role, that of a real-life princess, married to Prince Rainier of Monaco, living, with her suitably beautiful children by her royal spouse, in a fairy-tale castle above the Mediterranean.

And now the wheel has turned again, as artistic director Kevin Spacey has chosen for himself and his Old Vic Theatre the original version of the play, *The Philadelphia Story*. He had cast Rosemary Harris's beautiful daughter, Jennifer Ehle, as Tracy Lord, who brings a kind of contemporary concern about the merits of inherited wealth to the role, and himself as Dex, the rich ex-husband with no such worries.

But wafting around the rafters of the Old Vic was the ghost of Kate Hepburn, checking on her replacement, along with Grace Kelly, who, for all her reputation as an Ice Maiden (which was one of the reasons Alfred Hitchcock was so fond of her), had had a fairly wild time on stage and as a Hollywood star before she swapped Malibu for the Med.

David Niven told me my favourite Grace Kelly story, dating from the time she was engaged to Prince Rainier, but still in the States getting ready for her wedding. Niven, who lived on the French Riviera, was sharing an after-dinner drink in the royal palace at Monaco with his friend, the Prince. Both men were famously fond of beautiful women and they each had a large collection of present and former lovers. Niven, who was as wonderfully gossipy and funny in person as in the seemingly endless round of chat shows that he undertook in the 1970s to promote his bestselling volumes of autobiography, was something of a cad when it came to boasting of his sexual prowess.

Speaking man to man, through a haze of brandy, Rainier leaned forward in his leather armchair and in a conspiratorial voice said to Niven, 'Come on, you've had a lot of women. Who was the best you've ever had?'

More than a little drunk and careless, Niven replied, without hesitation, 'I think it was Grace—' Realising, even as he said the words, what a monumental blunder he was about to make, and with visions of being carted off to the Monaco prison, he immediately corrected himself: 'Grac-ie! Yes, Gracie Fields! Fabulous singer, great in bed!'

Had she known, Gracie Fields, who herself enjoyed the Mediterranean sun on the island of Capri, would no doubt have given one of her trademark chuckles, and said, 'Ta very much!'

Somewhere, in the rafters of the Old Vic, Grace and Kate are giggling over that one.

THEATRE OF BLOOD (IT'S THICKER THAN WATER)

NATIONAL THEATRE, 2005

There's a wonderful song by the American singer-songwriter Amanda McBroom called 'Two Below Errol Flynn', which is written from her own experience as the daughter of a movie star. I have always loved her, and that song, particularly a line where she sings of watching her father on television in films where he is younger than she is now. I too have that experience of seeing my father younger than I am – well, everybody's younger than I am now! – and it's always eerie.

One of Pa's favourite films was *Theatre of Blood*, in which he played a poodle-loving, camp theatre critic, one of several who were brutally murdered by a deranged actor out to kill all the critics who had given bad reviews to his Shakespearean performances. He killed each in the manner of a murder in Shakespeare's plays, so they were particularly bloody and particularly funny.

In 2005, the National Theatre mounted Lee Simpson and Phelim McDermott's stage version of this early 1970s MGM horror/drama/comedy. The actor Edward Lionheart was played in the film by Vincent Price and at the National by Jim Broadbent. What we discovered, when we saw it on stage, is that it is undeniably theatrical, set entirely in an old, decaying theatre.

Speaking as a theatre critic, sitting surrounded by the usual cohort of regular reviewers for all the major newspapers, I found that it was a curiously uncomfortable feeling to hear the

---

laughter of the audience (many of them well-known actors on a night off) at the hideous and gory discomfiture of assorted onstage critics being stabbed, impaled and otherwise dispatched in front of our eyes, largely thanks to illusionist Paul Kieve's skills.

It was also uncomfortable for me, since there was, in my mind's eye if not actually in the Lyttelton auditorium, a personal relationship between me and what was happening on stage. The stage design was topped by the image of a lion, a double tribute to Edward Lionheart and the lion mascot of MGM, the company responsible for the original film.

And in the role Pa plays in the film, the camp, poodle-loving critic and gourmet – performed wonderfully on stage by Bette Bourne – is killed by being force-fed the flesh of his two doggie 'babies' (shades of *Titus Andronicus*).

It was, to say the least, an actor's revenge dream come true, and a play packed with theatrical (and specifically National Theatre) in-jokes, but it had the effect of bringing back extraordinarily strong memories of the movie. And mine wasn't the only memory being tricked into seeing two actors in every role – the one currently playing and the one who played it first – because the part of the deranged actor's daughter and accomplice, Miranda Lionheart, was played by Rachael Stirling – looking uncannily like her mother, who had played the same part in the film.

I wondered, since Bette Bourne's critic died horribly, what my father would have made of it all. Miss Stirling didn't have to wonder about her parent, because there in the audience, beaming proudly, was the original Miranda – Dame Diana Rigg.

But the odd relationship between actors and critics continues. I once asked Pa what it was like to be an actor with a critic for a son. 'Well, darling,' he said, 'it's a bit like being a general in the Israeli Army and waking up to discover that your son is an Arab.'